THIRD CUSTOM EDITION

3DS
Animation Basics
MAX®

by Eric Regner
Autodesk Certified Trainer

Learning Solutions

New York   Boston   San Francisco
London   Toronto   Sydney   Tokyo   Singapore   Madrid
Mexico City   Munich   Paris   Cape Town   Hong Kong   Montreal

Pearson Learning Solutions, 501 Boylston Street, Suite 900, Boston, MA 02116
A Pearson Education Company
www.pearsoned.com

Printed in the United States of America

2 3 4 5 6 7 8 9 10 V011 14 13 12 11 10

000200010270569366

KW

ISBN 10: 0-558-64491-0
ISBN 13: 978-0-558-64491-8

CONTENTS

ACKNOWLEDGMENTS:

TOBY WATERS: Toby has been a huge help in putting together this book, and making sure it is up to date with the latest versions of Max. Thanks!

MY FAMILY: The support and encouragement they offer make anything possible.

ALSO OF MENTION: The students whom I have had the pleasure, and pain, of teaching in the last 5 years. Although they ranged in talent and desire, I have learned valuable lessons from every one of them. I only hope to see one of them in the credits of a great game, or movie, in the near future.

This text is a basic primer to learning animation in 3DS MAX. It is not a character animation book, but a general animation book meant to teach the basic animation tools to students prior to trying characters. When students have an understanding of the concepts and skills discussed in this book, they will have a firm foundation for moving on to more complex animation techniques.

If you are reading this book, you obviously have an interest in multimedia, animation, or the creative arts. To really become skilled in any creative field, you must practice. After you have practiced, practice some more. Art in any form, and animation is an art, requires passion. If you lack the passion for one discipline, or software, find another. Even those who were born oozing with talent need to put the hours in to develop their skills to a level an employer would be impressed with.

True artists never stop learning and honing their skills. They would do anything to spend more time doing what they love. How many aspiring actors wait tables in Hollywood while in acting school, or trying to become an actor?

Find a passion. If you really love doing something, chances are you are pretty good at it. If you develop this passion, and put in the time necessary to become great, you might be lucky enough to get paid to do what you love. I do!

THE MAX INTERFACE

Let's jump right in to the MAX interface! Below is a screenshot of 3DS MAX. Your interface may differ slightly in appearance, depending on your computer's operating system.

Following are the main areas of the screen that will be used during modeling. The areas not covered now will be covered in the animation sections.

NOTES

The color-coded screenshot below shows the major areas of the interface.

The color-coded graphic above shows the main areas of the screen dealt with in the modeling portion of these lessons. They are, by color:

- Yellow: Pull-down menus

- Green: Main Toolbar

- Cyan: Command Panels

- Magenta: Viewport Navigation Controls

- Red: Prompts, and coordinate type in area

- Orange: Viewports

- Blue: Graphite Modeling Tools

Take a look at each part of the interface in detail.

NOTES

PULL-DOWN MENUS:

If you are familiar with any other Windows or Mac OS software, you have used pull-down menus. In MAX they are: Application button and Quick Access toolbar, Edit, Tools, Group, Views, Create, Modifiers, Character, Reactor, Animation, Graph Editors, Rendering, Customize, MAXScript, and Help. Depending on what plug-ins or other tools you loaded into MAX, they may also include other items. Topics covered here will be the pull-down menus that are used first in the modeling lessons. They will be revisited and examined as needed.

The Application button functions as a typical Windows OS application "File" pull-down. However, it organizes the options into sub-groups. For example, the "New" sub-group contains the options for opening a whole new file, a new file which keeps the session settings and objects, or a new file which keeps settings, objects, and hierarchies. Simply clicking on the sub-group "New" will open the default "New" option, which is the first option in the list of the "New" sub-group.

Below are screenshots showing you the options available. Note that MAX describes the options for you.

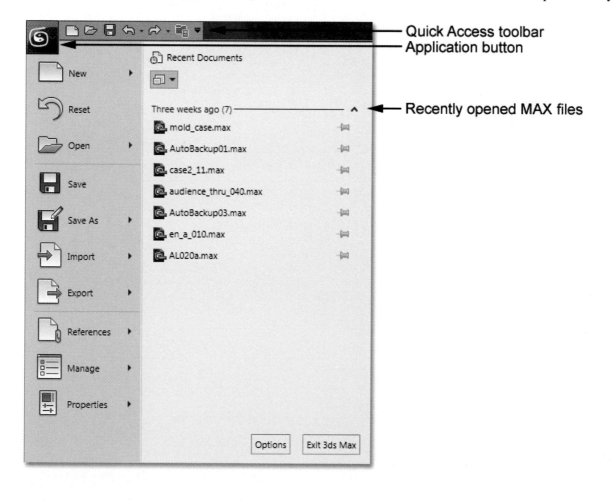

NOTES

NOTES

NOTES

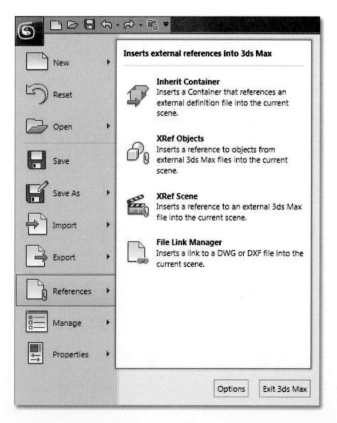

NOTES

NOTES

The edit menu contains tools to select and undo/redo commands.

Undo	Ctrl+Z
Redo	Ctrl+Y
Hold	Ctrl+H
Fetch	Alt+Ctrl+F
Delete	Delete
Clone	Ctrl+V
Move	W
Rotate	E
Scale	
Transform Type-In...	F12
Transform Toolbox...	
Select All	Ctrl+A
Select None	Ctrl+D
Select Invert	Ctrl+I
Select Similar	Ctrl+Q
Select Instances	
Select By	▶
Selection Region	▶
Manage Selection Sets...	
Object Properties...	

The Undo and Redo options work just like any other software. MAX, by default, saves 20 commands deep. This setting can be changed in the Customize menu.

Hold is a temporary save, used in conjunction with Fetch, to set the scene back to the Hold point.

Delete removes the currently selected object.

Clone creates a copy of the selected object.

Move enables the "Select and Move" tool.

Rotate enables the "Select and Rotate" tool.

Scale enables the "Select and Uniform Scale" tool.

Transform Type-In allows you to type in transform coordinates specific to the transform tool currently in use. The Transform Toolbox contains functions for easy object rotation, scaling, and positioning as well as for moving object pivots.

Select All selects all objects in the scene.

Select None de-selects everything in the scene.

Select Invert selects things that were previously unselected.

Select Similar allows you to select all similar objects.

Select Instances selects all instances of the current selection.

Select By gives you other ways of selecting objects.

Selection Region shows the options for selecting objects in the viewport.

Manage Selection Sets opens the Named Selection Sets dialog.

Object Properties opens the Object Properties dialog.

Let's move on the toolbars. The other pulldown menus are important, too. However they can be discussed as needed. Do not overlook the Help menu! The MAX help files are wonderful, as are the included tutorial files. Use them!

NOTES

THE MAIN TOOLBAR:

The tools are labeled (left to right): Select and Link, Unlink Selection, Bind to Space Warp, Selection Filter List, Select Object, Select From Scene, Selection Region Flyout, Window/Crossing Selection Toggle, Select and Move, Select and Rotate, Select and Scale Flyout, Reference Coordinate System, Selection Center Flyout, Select and Manipulate, Keyboard Shortcut Override Toggle, Snap Flyout, Angle Snap Toggle, Percent Snap Toggle, Spinner Snap Toggle, Edit Named Selection Sets, Named Selection Sets, Mirror, Align Flyout, Layer Manager, Graphite Modeling Tools, Curve Editor, Schematic View, Material Editor, Render Setup, Rendered Frame Window, Render Flyout.

The Main Toolbar resides beneath the pull-down menus. It contains the most-used tools for manipulating objects in MAX. The above graphic describes the tools. By default, the Graphite Modeling Tools button is enabled. As you can see, below the Main Toolbar, the Graphite Modeling Tools bar is open. To close this, simply toggle the Graphite Modeling Tools button in their Main Toolbar.

In the first exercises, concentration will be on the "transform" tools: Move, Rotate, and Scale.

THE COMMAND PANELS:

The Command Panels contain all the creation tools found in the pull-down menus, and more. They are a convenient place to both create and modify objects. To select the panels, simply click on the "tab" shown in the following graphic.

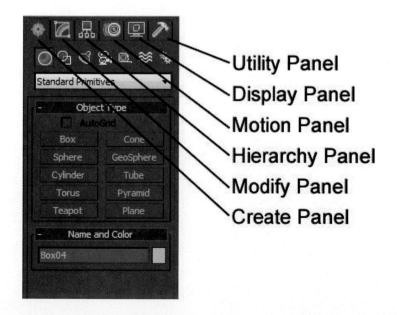

For the first few lessons, concentrate on the Create and Modify Panels. Take a look at the options in each:

NOTES

CREATE PANEL:

The Create Panel is where you start when creating anything for your scene. The look of the panel changes with each object type you choose.

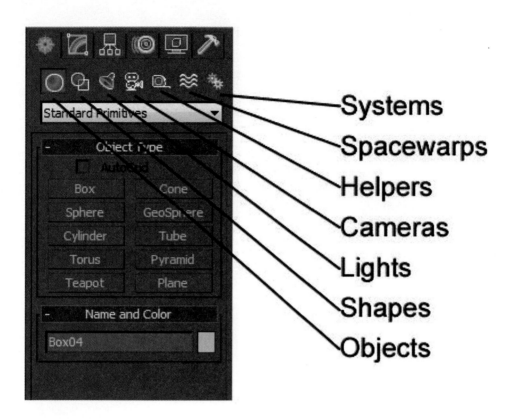

The Objects button allows you to create all sorts of 3D objects in the viewports. In the lab, you will create many different 3D primitive objects.

NOTES

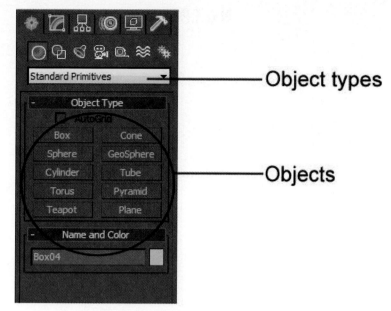

In the Objects area (above), notice that the Object Types list box shows many object types. When one of these object types is chosen, such as "Standard Primitives," the objects are available below as buttons. These buttons will change, depending on the object type chosen.

When objects have been created, you can change their parameters by using the Modify Panel.

THE MODIFY PANEL:

The Modify Panel allows changes to parameters of any object created. It also allows you to add "modifiers," such as Bend and Twist, to an object. Review the Modify Panel. The graphic below shows the Modify Panel after a 3D Primitive has been created (a box).

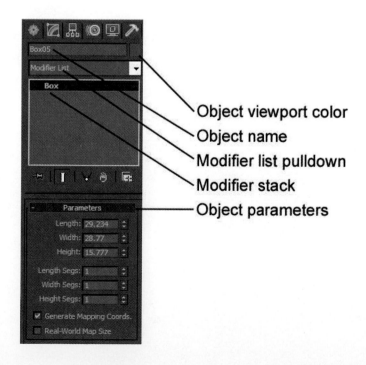

NOTES

The Viewport Color of the object shows that the box is purple. To change it, simply click the color chip.

The Object Name field can be edited (and should be edited) to name an object. This is very important to remember, as no one wants to have 100 boxes in the scene without intelligent names applied to them!

The Modifier List has a list of modifiers that can be applied to the object.

The Modifier Stack (discussed later) shows the "list" of modifiers applied to the object, in order.

The Object's Parameters allow you to modify the parameters. In this case, you can change the length, width and height of the box. The segments area will be discussed later.

THE VIEWPORTS:

The Viewports are where most of the work using MAX will be performed. When you first open MAX, you are given a four-viewport configuration, consisting of a Top, Front, Left, and Perspective views.

The above graphic shows the main features that you need to understand. The Viewport Name indicates which view is being used for that viewport. There are many available, including:

- top
- bottom
- left
- right
- front
- back

NOTES

- user
- perspective
- camera
- other "extended" viewports

The View Menu is also an important feature to control the display of the viewport. Try right-clicking on the View Menu and you will see the options. These will be covered later when objects are created.

The gold border is an indication of the current viewport. To make a different viewport active, try to get in the habit of right-clicking in another one. Although left-clicking will work fine, you will find that using left-click to activate another viewport will cancel the current selection when you are working. Use that right-click!

The viewport borders allow you to resize the viewports to suit your needs while working in MAX. To resize the viewports, left-click on the border and drag it around. You will notice the cursor changes when you move it over the borders.

The Grids are default construction grids that your objects will be created on. This will be obvious later in lab.

THE VIEWPORT NAVIGATION CONTROLS:

There are MANY ways to manipulate the way an object is displayed in the viewports. The first method is to use the Navigation Tools in the lower right hand corner of the interface.

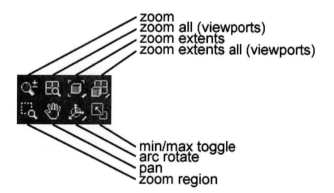

As with some of the other tools in the Main Toolbar, some of these buttons have little black arrows in their lower right hand corners. This indicates other options to the tool that you can access by left-clicking and holding the mouse button down.

These Viewport Navigation Controls change when different viewports are active. The figure above shows the controls for an orthogonal, perspective or User Viewport. Pay attention to what the controls look like when in a camera or spotlight viewport!

NOTES

CHAPTER ONE

ANIMATION BASICS

PREVIEW

To understand what animation is, and how it is done with 3DS MAX, we will first take a brief tour of the history of animation. This includes the 12 Principles of Animation, which should always be forefront in your mind when animating any sequence.

In the next section of this chapter, we will look at Time in MAX and set up a classic "bouncing ball" animation. This will give us the basics of how animation is performed in MAX.

In the final part of this chapter, we will animate a simple 3D object traversing an obstacle course.

TERMINOLOGY AND CONCEPTS

Persistence of Vision: The physiological ability of the eye to retain an image, and the brain to perceive motion from a series of images, played back in quick succession.

Keyframe: A frame in an animation where changes of an object's properties, such as position and rotation, were set by the animator.

Tween: From "In-Between": Frames in-between keyframes. In cell animation, a junior animator would draw the tweens, while the lead animator drew only the keyframes. In computer animation, tweens are calculated by the software based upon the keyframes the animator created, and the tangent types defined.

Principles of Animation: The 12 rules of animating, first developed by early Disney animators. The rules will help animators create more lifelike and interesting animation, no matter what the subject of the animation.

Time: For our purposes, time is measured in SMPTE (Society of Motion Picture and Television Engineers) units of hours, minutes, seconds, and frames. The number of frames per second of animation is set by the format it is to be delivered in. In 3DS MAX, the default time unit is frames, at an NTSC (National Television Systems Committee) standard frame rate of 30 frames per second.

Curve Editor: In MAX, the Curve Editor is a Track View mode which displays motion as function curves on a graph. These curves show the velocity, acceleration, and changes in properties over time. The Curve Editor also allows the animator to set tangent types (such as slowing down or speeding up) on the keyframes of the animation.

Tangents: Refers to the Curve Editor animation curves: The definition of how the tweens are calculated between keyframes of an animation. MAX, by default, assigns smooth tangents to keyframes. The animator can easily change between the tangent types (Custom/Bezier, Fast in/out, Slow in/out, Step, Linear and Smooth) in the Curve Editor.

Dope Sheet: In MAX, the Dope Sheet is a Track View mode which displays keyframes as a horizontal graph. The Dope Sheet is used to adjust the timing of the keyframes of an animation.

Trajectories Button: In MAX, the Trajectories Button in the Motion Panel allows us to visually see the path of translation of an object being animated. It also allows us to judge the speed of the object, as well as the tangent type assigned to a keyframe.

WHAT IS ANIMATION?

Animation, or the illusion of motion, is based upon the mechanism of the human eye and brain connection which allows us to see a sequence of images, played back in quick succession, as a single smooth motion. This mechanism is referred to as "persistence of vision".

In the early years of animation, moving characters, machines, etc. were hand drawn by animators on cells (named for the celluloid material they used). These drawings were then colored in, or inked to create full-color drawings. These were then layered with background art, and photographed to produce animations for film.

Planning the timing of each scene, and any associated voiceover, was accomplished using a dope sheet, or exposure sheet. Below is an example I have used from time to time. This is also available as a PDF file in the Chapter 1 folder on the CD-ROM.

SEQUENCE	SCENE				TITLE					SHEET
ACTION		DIAL	5	4	3	2	1	BG		CAMERA INSTRUCTIONS

NOTES

Once the timing was completed, the lead animators would draw the "key poses" or "key frames" of the animation, while junior animators drew the "in-betweens," or "tweens."

In the computer, using software such as Autodesk 3DS MAX, the animator creates the keyframes, and the computer creates the tweens. Of course, the animator has control over how the tweens are timed using the dope sheet and curve editor, and you model instead of draw, use materials instead of inking, and use virtual cameras and lighting for layering and backgrounds.

12 PRINCIPLES OF ANIMATION

Whether animating by hand, or using the computer, there are some basic principles you should thoroughly understand: Namely, the Principles of Animation. These principles apply to any object, character, etc. you will be animating.

I have seen animators list as many as 28, or as few as 10 principles of animation, but most sources speak in terms of 12. These 12 date back to the golden age of animation, and Frank Thomas and Ollie Johnston working at Disney in the early 1920s.

The principles of animation are:

1. Squash and Stretch
2. Anticipation
3. Staging
4. Straight Ahead Action & Pose to Pose
5. Follow Through & Overlapping Action
6. Slow in and out
7. Arcs
8. Secondary Action
9. Timing
10. Exaggeration
11. Appeal
12. Solid Drawing

Let's take a look at each in more detail.

Squash and Stretch

Squash and stretch is the indicator of the flexibility of an object. It is the action of an object changing shape when contacting and leaving a surface, while trying to retain its volume.

For example, think of a person's face when they begin to smile. The face flexes and muscles tighten, as the smile becomes larger. The face will retain its volume, but will stretch to show the action of the smile.

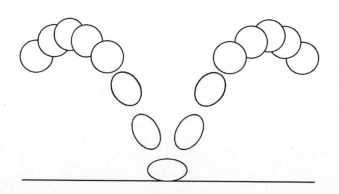

NOTES

Another example would be a bouncing ball. The ball will squash a bit when contacting a surface, but its volume will remain constant. Additionally, to add life to the ball it could stretch when "reaching" for the ground.

Anticipation

Anticipation

Before starting the flip, the box rotates in the opposite direction, and bends to save up enough energy to flip.

Anticipation is the preparation for action. When getting ready to jump into the air, a person crouches and tightens the leg muscles like compressing a spring. This can be thought of a storing energy for an action by moving in the opposite direction of the action.

Anticipation is used to set up the main action and should also be in proportion to the main action: Big action requires large anticipation! Check out the beginning of the animation "box-flip.avi" in the Chapter 1 folder on the CD-ROM.

Staging

Staging is presenting the scene so that the action is clearly understood by the audience. If a scene is staged properly, the mood, camera angle, and all aspects of the scene will help the audience understand what the action is. Staging is putting a scene in context.

Straight Ahead Action & Pose to Pose

Straight ahead animation refers to starting at the beginning of a sequence and animating "straight ahead" until the end. Pose to pose animation refers to animating the major action, or poses, and then filling in between the poses as needed.

Straight ahead action tends to be very spontaneous, but can easily get "out of hand," as there is no clear direction to follow. Pose to pose tends to look planned, and can be a bit too staged.

The best animation is usually a blend of both techniques, especially in computer animation. MAX has both methods available to the animator, and you will be using both in the exercises to follow.

NOTES

Follow Through & Overlapping Action

When the box lands after the flip, it has to catch itself and dissipate the energy of landing by overshooting the place where it landed.

Newton's laws of motion come into play in this principle!

The best way to understand this principle is to contrast it with Anticipation. If Anticipation sets up the action *before* the action takes place, Follow Through and Overlapping Action is what happens after the action. Again, look at the animation "box-flip.avi" in the Chapter 1 folder on the CD-ROM. This time, pay particular attention to the last part of the animation.

When a pitcher throws a ball, his arm continues to follow through after the ball has left his hand. The batter's swing continues after he has made contact with the ball he just hit. The forces required to impart energy on the ball cannot stop suddenly, so they overlap the main action of the ball leaving the hand or bat.

Another example is a loose-fitting shirt on a person walking. If this person stops quickly, the shirt will continue to move. There are many examples in real life. Can you think of a few more?

Slow in and out

Newton's laws of motion strike again!

Slow in describes an object taking time to "get up to speed." The motion has to overcome the object's inertia. Similarly slow out refers to an object decelerating and not abruptly coming to a stop when acted upon by friction, air resistance or other forces. The object's kinetic energy has to be dissipated.

Arcs

An arc describes the path objects take when moving in an expressive manner. Straight, linear motion is not very natural, and mainly exists only in man-made machines.

Think of the path your ankle takes when you walk. It does not move in a linear motion, but rather in an arc.

Secondary Action

Secondary action describes any actions that are not the main action. Secondary action reinforces the main action by adding details and depth to the motion.

For example, think of a bouncing ball. If the ball wiggles when bounced we perceive a soft, almost gelatin-like substance. The wiggle is secondary motion that reinforces the main action.

NOTES

Picture a sad person walking down a sidewalk. The action of walking is the primary motion, but what secondary actions would help convey the emotion of the character?

Timing

Timing gives weight to objects, and meaning to the animated movement.

A simple example would be the difference between a very heavy person and a smaller thin person walking together. The timing of their strides is a clue as to the weight of the person. Heavy objects move different than light ones due to taking more time to change directions, speed up, and slow down.

Another example would be a very happy person and a sad person walking. The emotion of the character would determine the speed of their walk.

Timing is one of the most important and critical aspects of animation.

Exaggeration

Exaggeration can be described as the "cartoony" look given to an animation. However, it is amazing just how much exaggeration is needed to create lifelike motion.

If you were to exactly measure every aspect of a person's walk and apply it to a character animation, it would still look stale and robotic. Exaggeration gives life to objects.

That being said, if you are not after that "cartoony" look, there has to be a balance between subtle exaggeration and pushing it too far. Over exaggeration can be disturbing, especially if everything in your scene is exaggerated.

Appeal

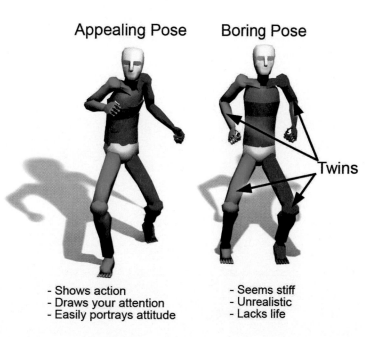

Appealing Pose   Boring Pose

Twins

- Shows action
- Draws your attention
- Easily portrays attitude

- Seems stiff
- Unrealistic
- Lacks life

Which of the above characters is more interesting? Appeal describes the "like-ability", or pleasing nature of the object, character, design, pose, color, or motion. Is the design of the scene, animation, and color attractive? Does the character have appealing poses when moving?

NOTES

When thinking about appeal, try to avoid what are called "twins," or symmetry in a pose. If both arms are posed in the same position, the character's appeal may suffer. At first, this seems to be a very subtle aspect of animation, but can lead to a very boring and stiff motion.

Solid Drawing or Design

Since we are using computer programs to model objects, solid drawing could be thought of as solid design.

Pay attention to design theory, composition, and solid design of the scenes, objects, and characters you animate. It boils down to animated artist expression, and not a boring, robotic feel to the motion.

TIME

Animation can be defined as a parameter or property changing over time, so before we can animate we must understand time. Different video and film standards define a second of time in varying frame rates. Below is a table of the various video and film frame rates.

Standard		Year Developed	Lines of Resolution	Horizontal Pixels	Vertical Pixels	Frame Rate	Locations used
NTSC	National Television System Committee	1953	525	720	480	29.97	North America, Japan, some Asian countries
PAL	Phase Analog Line	1960's	625	720	576	25	Western Europe, Australia, Africa, some Asian countries
SECAM	Systeme Electronique Couleur Avec Memoire	1960's	625	720	576	25	France, former French Colonies, some eastern European countries
35mm Film						24	Worldwide

For our use in this book, we will be referring to the NTSC DV video standard. In North America, NTSC video plays at 29.97 frames per second. For our purposes in MAX, we will use 30 frames per second. This means we must render 30 frames of a scene to create a single second of animation.

The default unit of time in MAX is frames. We can display time in various ways in MAX, but for now we will stick to frames. When MAX is started, the length of time on the timeline is 100 frames, giving us 3.33 seconds to work with. Let's take a look at the interface tools we will be using to animate with.

NOTES

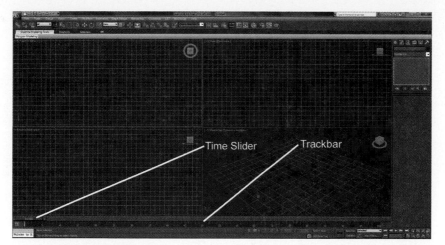

The figure above shows the Trackbar and the Time Slider. The Trackbar displays a timeline which is used to position the Time Slider when animating.

The figure below shows the Autokey and Setkey buttons. They are for creating straight ahead and pose to pose animation, respectively. We discussed these techniques previously in the 12 Principles of Animation section.

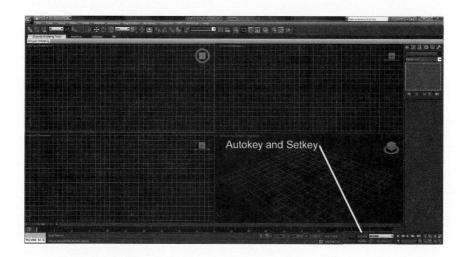

In the following exercise, we will use the Time Slider and the Autokey button to animate a bouncing ball.

NOTES

HANDS ON:
EXERCISE #1—"THE BIG BOUNCE"

THE GOAL:

On the CD-ROM, take a look at the file "ballbounce-finished.avi" in the Chapter 1 folder. There are a few things we need to pay attention to.

First, notice the shape of the trajectory of the ball. The trajectory is a series of arcs, which we discussed in the principles of animation section. The ball accelerates towards the ground, pulled by gravity. As it hits the stairs, it quickly rebounds and moves up into the next arc. At the top of the arc, the ball slows down, and very briefly stops before heading down again.

THE EXERCISE:

Let's load the "ballbounce-start.max" file from the Chapter 1 folder. Here you will find a staircase and ball ready for you to animate.

- Go to the Motion panel and turn on the "Trajectory" toggle.

This will allow us to visualize the motion as we animate. Now let's get started! Begin by turning on the autokey button. You should see the trackbar area turn red.

> **NOTE:** Be sure to turn on the autokey button when you want to save animation. Also be sure to turn it off when you are done! MAX will not save any animation without the autokey button on, and will animate any parameter changes when it is on!

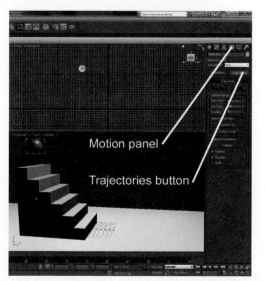

Motion panel

Trajectories button

- Move the time slider to frame 5, and then move the ball forward and down in the Front Viewport until it makes contact with the stair.

NOTES

- Move the time slider to frame 10, and move the ball up and forward, to approximately the position shown below

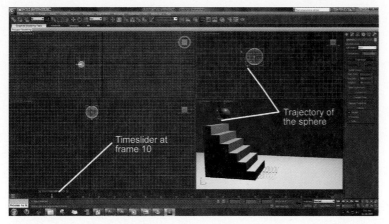

- Continue to move the time slider, and then move the ball, until you have animated the ball bouncing to frame 100. Using the playback controls, rewind the time slider to frame 0, and then playback your animation. You should see the ball bouncing through the trajectory for 100 frames.

What do you see that could be improved? The first, most obvious problem is that at each keyframe where the ball contacts the ground it seems to "slide" rather than hit and return sharply. The trajectory seems to be a sine wave, rather than a series of arcs meeting at points.

We want to get our trajectory to look like the second picture.

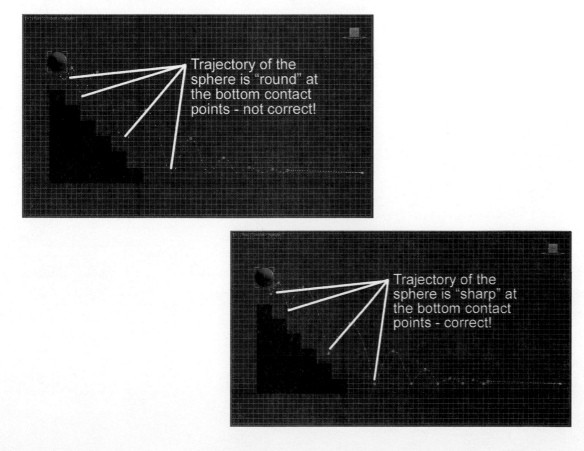

NOTES

- Select the ball, and go to the Track View Curve Editor (curve editor), from the Graph Editor pull-down menu. You should see something like the picture below.

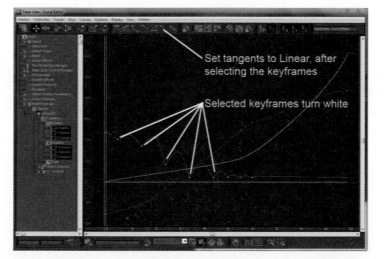

What we see in the figure above is the position keyframes, and their motion curves, we created by moving the sphere with the autokey button on. You should notice the Sphere01 object has a yellow highlight because it is selected. The X, Y, and Z positions are also highlighted, because we animated the sphere's position.

The next thing to notice about the figure above is that there are three colored curves shown: Red, Green, and Blue. These correspond to the X, Y, and Z position curves, respectively. By clicking on the "Z Position" words in the left side of the Curve Editor, we can isolate the Z Position curve which should look like exactly the trajectory we were using in the Viewport.

- Select the bottom keyframes of the Z position curve (they will turn white when selected) and then click on the "set tangents to linear" button. Your curve should look like the figure below.

- Close the Curve Editor, and playback your animation. It should look much better, as the ball sharply hits the ground and quickly rebounds up into the air.

As we have just seen, one of the uses of the curve editor is to control the "tangents," or curvature in and out of each keyframe. For a bouncing ball contacting stairs, we needed to set the contact keyframes to a linear tangency so they contact and rebound sharply.

NOTES

TIMING:

Play the animation back a few times. Is the ball bouncing at the right speed? Does your ball look heavy, or light? What's the difference between the way a heavy ball bounces and the way a light ball bounces? These are not easy questions, and creating an animation showing proper weight is not either!

Timing has a huge effect on the feeling of weight in an animation. There are a few different ways to change the timing of our bouncing ball. The best place to adjust timing is in the Track View – Dope Sheet (dope sheet), from the Graph Editor pull-down menu. Select the ball object, and open the dope sheet. You should see something similar to what's shown below.

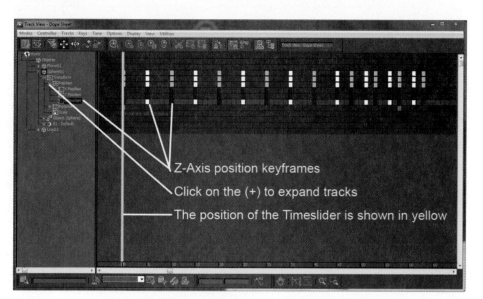

Z-Axis position keyframes
Click on the (+) to expand tracks
The position of the Timeslider is shown in yellow

The ball object is highlighted on the left side of the dope sheet window. The boxes on the graph are the keyframes you created earlier. If you cannot see the position track, you can click on the "+" sign to the left of the object or track. This expands the tracks in a similar manner to the Windows Explorer interface when you are examining the contents of folders on your computer.

First, let's see the effect of speeding up the ball's animation.

- Move your Time Slider to frame 0. (You may need to re-arrange your workspace a bit by dragging the Dope Sheet window up to see the time slider.) This should move the double blue lines in the dope sheet to frame 0.

- Select all the keyframes in the Dope Sheet by dragging a window around them: They should all turn white.

- Choose the Scale Keys button. With the Scale Keys button selected, click and drag on any of the selected keyframes in the Dope Sheet. You should see them scale in time, but keep their relative timing to each other. Scale the keys so the animation goes from frame 0 to frame 50. Close the Dope Sheet.

What did we just do? We made the 100-frame long animation of the ball take place in 50 frames, increasing the speed of the ball by a factor of 2. Play the animation, and you should see the effects.

Save your MAX file to a folder on your hard drive.

NOTES

Let's review what we did.

POSITION OF THE BALL:

Open your saved file, or open the file "ballbounce-finished.max" from the Chapter 1 folder. Select the ball and go the Motion tab of the Command Panel. Click on the Parameters button. Next, click on the Assign Controller roll-out. You should see the options shown below.

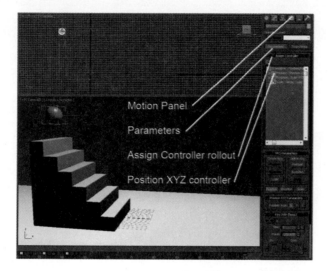

Before you started to animate the ball, MAX had assigned a default controller, or way of animating the ball. The default Position controller, or the way MAX defined the position of the ball, was by a Position XYZ controller. This allows us to keyframe the position of the ball in three axes: X, Y, and Z.

CURVE EDITOR:

When we looked at the trajectory of the ball in the Curve Editor, we see motion curves for the X, Y, and Z axes (the red, green, and blue curves, respectively). These were created when we animated the ball, and were generated because of MAX's default position controller, Position XYZ.

In the Curve Editor, we were able to modify the way MAX "tweened" our animated keyframes, by setting tangent point types. Depending on the tangent type we choose, we can Accelerate, Decelerate, or Step in to, or out of, our keyframes.

The Curve Editor and its companion, the Dope Sheet, allow us to change almost any aspect of our animation. In fact, they can be used to create animation without seeing the viewports at all. Try it!

DOPE SHEET:

The Dope Sheet allows us to retime our animation. Depending on where our Time Slider is positioned, and what keys we have selected, we can move and scale the time between keyframes. We can also speed up a section of the animation, while leaving other sections untouched.

NOTES

EXERCISE #2 — OBSTACLE COURSE

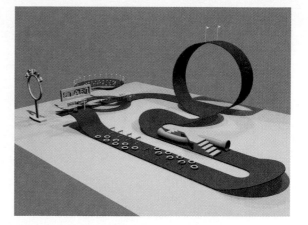

THE GOAL:

On the CD-ROM, open the file "obstaclecourse-finished.avi" in the Chapter 1 folder. You should see a red ball navigating through part of the 3D obstacle course.

You will be using what you just learned in the previous exercise, only this time you will be animating in all three directions, X, Y, and Z.

THE EXERCISE:

Let's load the "obstaclecourse-start.max" file from the Chapter 1 folder. You will notice that there are 300 frames in our trackbar. This file was created knowing we would need extra frames to animate the obstacle course. Additional time can be added at any time by using the Time Configuration dialog.

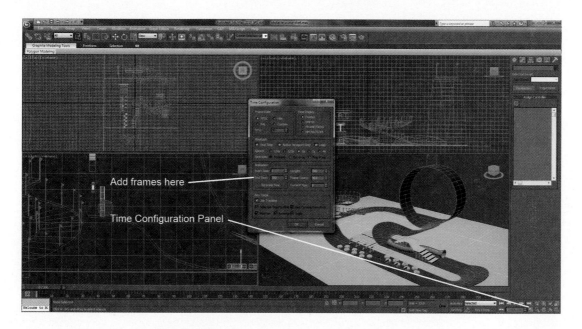

Add frames here

Time Configuration Panel

When you click on the Time Configuration button, it opens a dialog box that allows us to change the active time segment shown in the trackbar. To add time to your animation, as was done in this exercise, we simply typed 300 frames as the end time.

You should be aware that the time configuration panel is non-destructive when using the start and end frames. Non-destructive means it will not delete keyframes. For example, if you have already animated 300 frames of this obstacle course and then change the active time segment to start at 0 and end at 30, it will not delete your keyframes. It simply displays frames 0 through 30 of your animation.

Let's get started!

- Go to the motion panel and turn on Trajectories. This feature of MAX will be extremely valuable in this exercise.

NOTES

- Select "Character 1" and activate your left Viewport. You may want to zoom in a little so that you can easily see the object and the track surface we are going to make it move along.

- Move your Time Slider to frame 5, and activate autokey.

- With your Select and Move Tool, position Character 1 half way down the first sloped portion of the track surface.

- Move your Time Slider to frame 10, and use the Select and Move Tool to position the character at the bottom of the slopes.

> **NOTE:** At this point, do not be concerned with the position of Character 1 with respect to the tires being offset. We will be fixing this later. Additionally, you will notice that Character 1 is going through the curved slope. We will be using the Curve Editor to fix this, too!

- Move your Time Slider to frame 15, and move Character 1 up above the tire, but still slightly in front of it.

- Move your Time Slider to frame 20, and move Character 1 down on top of the first tire.

Repeat this and down keyframing every five frames until the character lands on the track after the last tire (if done in five-frame increments, your character should land in front of the first hurdle on frame 100).

- Using the trajectories as a guide, go back and readjust Character 1's position as necessary from the Left Viewport.

> **NOTE:** Be sure to adjust the position at existing keyframes! There is no need to add additional keyframes.

When you are finished, you should have something that looks similar to the figure below.

NOTES

Next, we will fix the contact keyframes when Character 1 hits the tires. As in the last exercise, the keyframes that make contact with the ground need to be set to linear tangency. While we are at it, let's also fix the problem with Character 1 moving through the slope of the track in the first 2 keyframes.

- Select the object Character 1, and open the Curve Editor. Expand the levels of Character 1 so you see the Z Position (Character 1>Transform>Position>Z Position). You may have to pan down the list of scene objects to see the yellow-highlighted object. Resize your curve editor window and viewport so that your interface looks like the figure below.

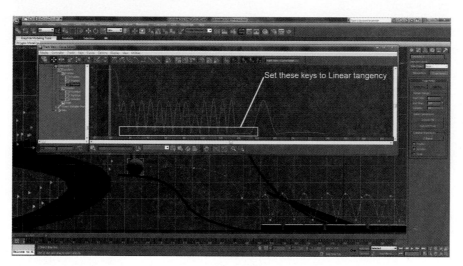

- Select all of the lowest keys (keys closest to 0) and set tangents to linear.

- Use the Bezier handles on the first two keys to adjust the trajectory curve to match the curve of the track's slope (see figure above).

- From the Top Viewport, start from frame 0 and adjust the character's position on the X axis to keep Character 1 inside the offset row of tires. Again, take care to have the autokey button active, and change the position on the X axis only on existing keys!

You should have a trajectory similar to the figure below.

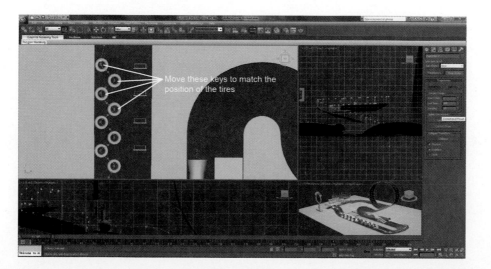

NOTES

- Continue your animation of Character 1 through the hurdles, around the corner, and through the blue offset tube.

Use the same technique of animating the rough positions, and then correcting errors at existing keyframes. Use the curve editor and tangent types to fix the motion through curved sections, and use linear tangency when Character 1 bounces into and off of objects.

Save your work! If you would like to see a completed animation through the blue offset tube, open the "obstaclecourse-finished.max" file from the Chapter 1 folder on the CD.

Let's review what we have done.

As in the first exercise, we were able to animate the position (and rotation, if you wanted to) of Character 1 due to a position XYZ controller which was applied by default in MAX.

In this exercise, we animated two axes in one view, and then modified the position keyframes to correct the position on the third axis. We then used the curve editor to change tangents, and adjusted the Bezier handles on a keyframe to match the track surface between keyframes.

CHAPTER SUMMARY

Any animation you perform in MAX is due to the animation controller(s) assigned. MAX assigns a default controller to each animation track. Moving and rotating an object using the transform tools is possible because of the default position and rotation controllers in MAX. The default position controller is a "Position XYZ," and the default rotation controller in the "Rotation XYZ." These controllers place Bezier tangents on the keyframes you create, which can be edited and modified through the curve editor.

You should know how to perform transform animation, or animating rotation and position using the transform tools in MAX. This consists of setting up time in the Time Configuration panel, moving the Time Slider, and setting the position and rotation keys when needed.

The Curve Editor allows us to change the keyframe properties of any animated parameter, and displays the information as function curves. Each track of animation, such as the position X, position Y, and position Z, each have their own keyframe curve showing the changes to the animated parameters of the object. You can change the keyframe value and tangent types of each keyframe on each animation track. There are many other powerful features of the curve editor, some of which will be covered later in this text.

The Dope Sheet allows us to retime animation keyframes, as well as change the values of the keyframes, and displays the information as a horizontal graph. The Dope Sheet is analogous to the exposure sheet in traditional animation.

REVIEW QUESTIONS

- Which of the 12 Principles of Animation be addressed in the curve editor?

- How can the position of the time slider affect the timing of keyframes in the Dope Sheet? (Hint: Try scaling selected keys with the time slider set at the first key and the last key of the animation.)

NOTES

- Why would you want to rough-out the position of an object you are animating, and fine-tune the motion later? (Hint: Think in terms of workflow and tasks needed to perform the animation.)

- What types of tangents are available in the Curve Editor? What does each tangent type do?

- Can you create a keyframe in the Curve Editor? If so, how?

BEYOND THE BASICS

- Try animating the Obstacle Course again, using the Flex modifier on Character 1. Flex provides secondary motion, but can cause your object to overshoot its position or rotation.

- Re-animate the bouncing ball, and try giving "weight" to the ball to make it look like a bowling ball. Create a second ball, and animate it to behave like a tennis ball.

- Add an FFD modifier to the bouncing ball to animate squash and stretch.

- Complete the obstacle course by animating both Character 1 and Character 2. Animate them finishing the course at the same time (a tie). Use the Dope Sheet to change the results of the race.

NOTES

CHAPTER TWO

RENDERING ANIMATIONS & ANIMATION CONSTRAINTS

PREVIEW

This chapter will continue introducing tools for animating. Constraints like the Look-at, Path, and Link constraints will be used to animate in a different way than with the transform tools.

You should already be aware of how to render a still image from MAX, but we will start the chapter with a discussion of how to render an animation. There are a few options to be aware of, like the CODEC with which you will render an AVI file.

TERMINOLOGY AND CONCEPTS

Rigging: Rigging refers to the process of building controls for the animator to use when animating the scene. It usually involves building and connecting the parts of a scene, and defining how objects move.

Controller Types: There are four main types of controllers in MAX: Transform, position, rotation, and scale controllers. Position controllers apply to the position only, rotation controllers control rotation only, etc. Controllers can be added in the Curve Editor, Dope Sheet, and Motion Panel.

Rendering: The action of turning the vector MAX file into a raster image with materials, lighting, and effects applied.

CODEC: COmpression/DECompression algorithm. CODEC refers to the compression type added to a video file. There are many CODEC's that are used with AVI and MOV file types, and it is important to understand what they are. If you create an AVI or MOV file with a CODEC on your computer, you will need that CODEC to playback the video file on another computer.

Hierarchy: A linked "chain" of objects (think of the song "The foot bone's connected to the shin bone, the shin bone's connected to the thigh bone…"). A hierarchy, and the way the objects are linked within it, define how objects will animate.

HANDS ON:
RENDERING ANIMATIONS:

Rendering an animation is very similar to rendering a still image. Let's take a look at the Render Setup dialog box. Open the dialog box by hitting the [F10] key. You should have the default settings, as shown below.

Time Output: What frames do you want to render?

Output Size: How big will each frame be?

Options: Any special requests?

Render Output: Filename, filetype, CODEC?

Final Settings: Which view to render?

We will focus our attention on the Common Tab. First, look at the Time Output section. Instead of the Single option, an animation requires multiple frames.

The first option is to render the "Active Time Segment," which refers to the length of time you have in the track-bar. The next option is to render a "Range" of frames, which allows us to check certain parts of animation. Next, we can specify the exact "Frames" we want to render. Note that we can render single frames separated by commas, or a range of frames using a hyphen.

Additionally, we have the option to render "Every Nth Frame," when rendering the active time segment or range. This is commonly used to render frames for use in Flash, or in animated GIF files for the web. For example, if my active time segment was 100 frames, and I chose to render every fifth frame, I would end up with 21 frames (don't forget frame "0"!): That's (100/5)+1.

NOTES

The next area of interest is the output size. This is a measure of the image's width and height in pixels. First, let's look at the list of presets available to us. The pull-down list, which now shows "Custom," contains many different presets used for Video, Film, HDTV, etc. If you were rendering for NTSC DV Video, you could simply choose the preset, and the entire output size section would be set up for you.

The Custom setting allows us to specify everything about the rendered animation. The Width and Height parameters are self-explanatory, and the Image Aspect is a ratio of the width divided by the height. The Pixel Aspect is not quite as obvious. Pixel Aspect ratio is the width of a single pixel divided by its height. The two main settings for Pixel Aspect are 0.9 and 1. If the Pixel Aspect is 0.9, you must be rendering for NTSC video and playback on a television, VHS or DVD device. For playback on a computer, or other formats of film and video, the pixel aspect should be 1.

The Options area of the render dialog is for special render options applied at render time. For instance, you can turn off Atmospheric effects and other Effects to quickly check the animation without taking time to calculate these effects. You can also turn on a video-legal color check, which will (by default) flag non-legal video colors with black. Options for this Video Color check can be found in the pull-down menus, under Customize > Preferences > Render tab.

The other notable Option is the Render to Fields checkbox. If your animation is destined for video, turning this feature on is desirable. Video is not actually whole frames, but rather two interlaced fields. These fields are created by rendering every other horizontal line of the frame, and compositing it with the other, opposite field line. Try rendering a frame with this setting on, and you will see better what I am describing.

The next parameter is the Render Output section: This where you will specify the video file type, as well as the compression for the file. There are two major categories of rendered animations. The first is a movie file, such as an AVI or QuickTime MOV file. These files are created as a single compressed movie, made from the individual rendered frames.

When you choose the option to render to a movie file, you are going to be asked to decide what CODEC to use to compress your movie. CODEC stands for COmpression/DECompression, and refers to the compression and decompression algorithm used to encode your movie. Of course, these movie files can be made without compression (no CODEC) for use in other applications like video editing or compositing software.

You must be very careful with your choice of CODEC. If you compress a movie in a CODEC that your client does not have, they will be unable to play it back, or use it in their editing or compositing software. Be sure to ask!

Additionally, some CODECs require certain color depths and resolutions, or do not offer the ability to render 32-bit files. Others work better with certain colors or even different operating systems on the PC. I have some simple suggestions that will help guide you to success. They are:

- If you are going to video or DVD, use the NTSC settings, and render to a DV CODEC.

- If you are going to post-process in an editor, or in compositing software, use no compression. These files will be large, but it is not recommended to compress from MAX, and re-compress from your editing package. You will end up with a pixilated and very ugly end result!

- If you are going to the Mac, use a QuickTime MOV. If it's to be post-processed, use no compression.

- If you want to play back the animation on the computer or a Mac from a hard drive, use a QuickTime MOV, 640x480, and use a Sorenson 3 CODEC. If the correct version of QuickTime is loaded, the file will play.

NOTES

- If the animation is to be played on a PC hard drive, AVI is a good choice. Try 640x480, and either an Indeo 3.2 or Cinepak CODEC. Both Indeo and Cinepak are common CODEC's, and were included with Windows from Win95 through XP.

- If the animation is to be played from CD-ROM, use the above two recommendations, but stick to a resolution of 320x240, or 640x480.

The second way to output animations is to render them to individual still frames. This may sound strange at first, but read on!

Rendering to still frames has only one possible disadvantage: Large amounts of disk space may be needed to store the frames, depending on the format. However, rendering to still images has many advantages:

- If you are rendering all night, and the power goes out on frame 1003, any frames you have rendered up to that point are saved. If you were rendering an AVI, the file isn't "written" until the last frame is rendered.

- Network rendering is only practical with still images. Each machine on a network can generate frames for the animation if it is rendered to stills. If you try to render a movie with network rendering, the whole movie is sent to a single machine.

- Editing and compositing software accept a still image sequence as input. They treat the sequence just like an AVI.

- Still image file types support 32 and even 48-bit color depth. Most movie formats cannot handle alpha channel, let alone 48 bit HDRI images.

Finally, the render dialog box has some final settings to be aware of. MAX will automatically make the current viewport the default render viewport. At the bottom of the render dialog box, you can choose the viewport to render. You can also avoid the frustration of accidentally rendering the wrong viewport by locking the viewport to be rendered.

EXERCISE #1—THE PATH CONSTRAINT AND LOOKAT CONSTRAINT

THE GOAL:

In the figure below, we want to make the roller coaster car ride on the tracks of the roller coaster. We will also make the camera on the camera tower follow the coaster car around the track.

THE EXERCISE:

Let's load the "rollercoaster-start.max" file from the Chapter 2 folder. This file contains a coaster car, "Car 1", with the wheels already linked to the car. There is also a completed roller coaster track, rails, and supports.

NOTES

- From the Select from Scene dialog box, ("H" shortcut key) select the "Car Path" shape.

This shape was used to create the rails and supports for the roller coaster, as well as to distribute the "wooden supports" around the track. As you can see, it is in the center of the rails. Also of note is the position of the "First Vertex." The First Vertex of a shape is not only important when lofting, it is also important when using path constraints.

THE PATH CONSTRAINT:

- Select the object "Car 1." From the Animation pull-down menu, choose "Constraints > Path Constraint." You should see a dashed line that acts like a rubber band.

- Although you could try to click on the "Car Path" in the viewport, it is much easier to hit "H" to bring up the Select from Scene dialog box, and choose "Car Path."

You should notice that Car 1 has been moved to the path, and it is currently located at the first vertex of the path. The command panel has also been switched to the motion panel, and the position controller has been changed. We know that the Position XYZ controller is the default controller, but it has been replaced by a Position List controller, which contains the original controller plus the Path Constraint controller.

- Drag the time slider, and you will notice that Car 1 follows the path, but its orientation does not change.

- To fix this problem, go to the motion panel. Pan down to the Path Parameters roll-out. Click the "Follow" checkbox. Car 1 should now be riding the rails!

That was easy, but there are some important points to discuss about what we just did.

First, and most important, is the fact that the Path Constraint is a Position Controller. By adding the constraint to Car 1, we replaced the original controller with a list controller that contains the original Position XYZ and the new Path Constraint controllers.

Second, we can see the car has been animated for us without having to turn on the autokey button. The Path Constraint applied the animation.

- Select Car 1 again, and you will see that the trackbar has two keyframes defined at frames 0 and 800.

- Be sure you can see the Path Parameters roll-out in the motion panel, and select Car 1. You will see that the trackbar has two keyframes defined at frames 0 and 800.

- Drag the time slider while watching the "Path Options: % Along Path" spinner in the modify panel.

When you assigned the Path Constraint to Car 1, MAX assumed you wanted Car 1 to start at the first vertex and end at the first vertex over the 800 frames that were defined in the time configuration dialog. These are very important points to remember when you use the path constraint!

- Save your file to a folder on your hard drive.

THE LOOKAT CONSTRAINT:

- Select "TV Camera" and right-click in the Left viewport. Type "C" to change the Left viewport into a Camera viewport, looking through the TV Camera.

NOTES

- Using the Top and Front viewports, rotate the TV Camera until you can see Car 1 in the middle of the TV Camera viewport. See the figure below.

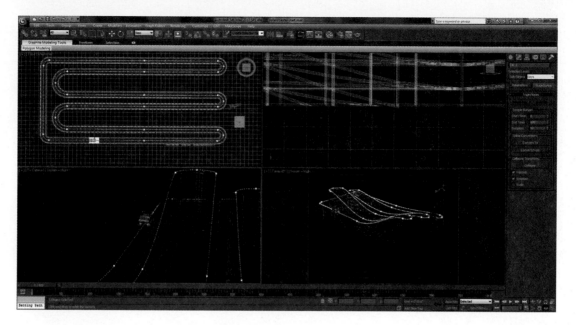

- Be sure that TV Camera is still selected, and go to the Animation pull-down menu. Choose "Constraints > LookAt Constraint". As with the path constraint, you should see the rubber band dashed line.

- Click on Car 1, and the TV Camera Viewport will look almost straight down. Don't Panic!

As with the Path Constraint, when we added the LookAt Constraint the motion panel became active. If you look at the LookAt Constraint roll-out (pun intended), you will see a checkbox labeled "Keep Initial Offset."

- Activate the Keep Initial Offset, and the TV Camera will return to the position you originally set for it.

- Drag the time slider, and you will see that the TV Camera follows Car 1 around the rails of the roller coaster.

- Save your file.

Let's review some of the important aspects of the LookAt Constraint.

We rotated and positioned the TV Camera before adding the LookAt Constraint to make it easier to apply the constraint. If we did not set up the initial position, we would need to use the Set Orientation button in the LookAt Constraint roll-out in the motion panel.

- Open your saved file, or the "rollercoaster-finished.max" file in the Chapter 2 folder on the CD-ROM.

If you look at the TV Camera in the MAX viewports, you will see a light blue line sticking out of the camera. This is the "Viewline" of the LookAt Constraint. It allows you to see the direction vector that the constraint is using.

Lastly, take a look at the Assign Controller roll-out of the motion panel (be sure the TV Camera is still selected!). You will notice the original Euler XYZ (Euler is pronounce like "oiler") controller has been saved under a Rotation List controller, along with the LookAt Constraint we added.

NOTES

EXERCISE #2—THE LINK CONSTRAINT

In this lab, we will learn how to animate a link to an object. MAX does not allow us to use the Autokey button with the Select and Link button in the main toolbar. To animate linking, we need the Link Constraint.

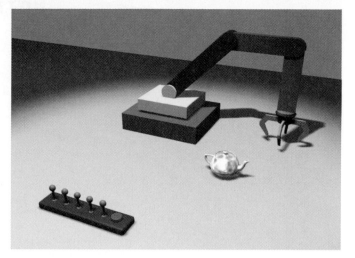

To see the animation we are going to create, view the "linkconstraint-finished.avi" file in the Chapter 2 folder. You will see a remote controlled crane that picks up a teapot, moves it to another location, and sets it down again. You will see how to set up this remote controlled crane later in Chapter 3.

Let's get started.

- Open the file "linkconstraint-start.max" from the Chapter 2 folder.

Before we begin, let's see what has been done for us. Select "Control Stick 1," select the rotation tool, and change the coordinate system to Local. Rotate the Control Stick 1 in the local X direction, and you will see the crane spin around. Each of the Control Sticks (1 through 5) have local X rotation connected to different parts of the crane. The Control Knob has local X rotation wired to the Claw Base rotation. Experiment with these controls for a while to become familiar with their use.

- Select "Control Stick 1," "Control Stick 2," "Control Stick 3," "Control Stick 4," "Control Stick 5," and "Control Knob." Click in the Create Named Selection Set field, type "controls," and hit [enter]. See the figure below.

Select these control objects and create a named selection set

This makes a named selection set which includes all of the objects we will use to animate with. To select all of these controls at once, use the pull-down arrow on the right of the field. This will become useful later!

- Return the crane to a neutral position, away from the teapot.

NOTES

- Select "Teapot01", and go to the motion panel. In the Assign Controller roll-out, click on "Transform:Position/Rotation/Scale" (on the words themselves: they should become highlighted) and then on the Assign Controller button. See the figure below.

- In the Assign Controller Dialog, choose the Link Constraint. This will replace the Position, Rotation, and Scale controllers with a "Transform: Link Constraint" controller.

- Be sure your Time Slider is on frame 0. In the "Link Params" roll-out of the motion panel, click on the "Link to World". You should see the table in the roll-out add a target of World at frame 0.

- Turn on the Autokey button, and move your time slider to frame 15. Using the local coordinate system, rotate the control sticks to position the crane's claw above the teapot. Use Control Stick 5 to open the claw, too.

- Move your Time Slider to frame 30, and position to crane's arm and claw around the teapot. Do not close the claw yet!

- Move the Time Slider to frame 40, and close the claw around the teapot.

- Go to the Named Selection Set filed, and choose "controls." You should see all 6 controls highlight. Next, right-click on the time slider to open the Create Key dialog box and create a Rotation Key for the selected objects at frame 40. Click OK.

- Select Teapot 01. Go to the motion panel and turn on the "Add Link" button by clicking on it. Next, click on one of the claws on the crane. You should see another target added (one of the 4 claws), at frame 40.

- TURN OFF THE "ADD LINK" BUTTON!

NOTES

- Move the Time Slider to frame 55, and be sure the Autokey button is on. Use the control sticks to animate the crane arm lifting and moving the teapot to another location. Be sure the arm is still holding the teapot in the air.

You should see the teapot move with the claw, as you animate the crane's arm.

- Move the Time Slider to frame 70, and set position the teapot back down on the grey surface using the Control Sticks 1–5. Be sure NOT to open the claws yet!

- Select the "controls" named selection set, and right-click on the Time Slider. Create a rotation key for the controls at frame 70.

- Select Teapot 01, and click on the "Link to World" button in the "Link Params" roll-out of the motion panel. You should now see three links, as shown in the figure below.

- Move your Time Slider to frame 80, and open the claws using "Control Stick 5."

- Move the Time Slider to frame 95 and move the crane arm up away from the teapot using the control sticks.

- Save your file.

Let's review what we just did.

Link constraints allow you to animate links in a hierarchy. You can animate the linking and unlinking of an object to another at points in time. When you "Link to World," you have returned an object to its original unlinked state (you linked to nothing).

NOTES

When linking and unlinking an object to a hierarchy with a link constraint, creating a keyframe for all members of the hierarchy is highly recommended. If you see strange and mysterious motion of the linked object after you have linked it to the world, you may not have created a keyframe for an object in the hierarchy.

For example, if the Teapot on the crane exercise moves after frame 70 when you move the crane arm, you probably forgot to create a keyframe for a part of the crane arm at frames 40 or 70.

SUMMARY

Constraints change the way you interact with objects when animating them. If you add a new position controller (like a path constraint) to an object, you cannot directly animate the object's position with the Select and Move tool. Likewise, the LookAt Constraint is a rotation controller. Direct rotation animation will not work once it is added.

The Link Constraint is the only way to animate hierarchical changes. The Link constraint is a "transform controller", meaning all positional, rotational and scaling aspects are controlled by another object in the hierarchy.

REVIEW QUESTIONS

- What still image types will MAX render to? Movie file types?
- Many compositing programs, like After Effects and Combustion, can import RPF filed from MAX. What makes RPF files different than JPG, TIF, TGA, etc.?
- What are 24, 32 and 48 bit images? What is Alpha Channel?
- How do you remove a path constraint (path controller) from an object? (Hint: It is not done by deleting it!)
- What types of constraints and controllers are available as position controllers? Rotation controllers? Scale controllers? Which category (position, rotation, or scale) does the link constraint belong to?

BEYOND THE BASICS

- Try using a path constraint, but use multiple paths. Try to get an object to use two circles as paths to get a figure-eight motion.

- Can you think of a way to animate an object following a path, but also having its vertical position controlled by an audio position controller? Hint: There are a few ways to do this. One way is by using a dummy object with a path constraint, which has the object linked to the dummy. The object will have the audio position controller. The second way is with a list controller. Be sure to try the MAX User Reference!

NOTES

CHAPTER THREE

WIRE PARAMETERS

PREVIEW

In the previous chapter, you discovered how to animate links using the link constraint, have an object follow a path, and control one object's rotation with another object using a look-at constraint. However, there are other ways to "link" or control one object with another.

Wiring, or Wire Parameters, is/are an extremely powerful tool for setting up complex animated relationships between two objects, or even controlling many parameters with a single object.

Confused? Well maybe now, but "confused" will become "impressed" by the time you finish this chapter.

TERMINOLOGY AND CONCEPTS

Freeze Rotation: When you select an object, and use the [ALT]+right-click, the animation quad menu shows a command to "freeze rotation." This command splits the current Euler XYZ controller into a list controller with the original "Initial Pose Euler XYZ" controller and a new "Keyframe XYZ: Euler XYZ." In essence, this allows you to "zero out" any rotation you used to position an object, and lets you control rotations from the current position. VERY important when using wire parameters!

Wire Parameters: Wire Parameters, and the Wire Parameters Dialog box, allow you to connect any animatable parameter of one object to any animatable parameter of another object. The easiest way to access the Wire Parameters command is from the quad menu (by right-clicking).

Hierarchy: A linked set of objects, obeying a parent–child relationship. In other words, when Object 1 is linked to Object 2, Object 2 is the parent and Object 1 is the child. When the parent is moved, the child follows. The child, however, can still move independently of the parent.

Reference Coordinate System: In MAX, you can use different coordinate systems for moving, rotating, and scaling objects. The coordinate system can be changed in the main toolbar. For this chapter, we will be using the Local Coordinate System exclusively.

NOTES

HANDS ON:

THE GOAL:

On the CD-ROM, open the file "crane-finished.max" in the Chapter 3 folder.

Select the Rotate tool, and then change the rotation to the local coordinate mode. You must choose the Rotate tool before changing the coordinate system!

Let's see what we are going to do in this lab. Select the leftmost control stick, and rotate it on the local X axis. The crane base spins. Select and rotate each control stick on its X axis, and a different part of the crane moves. Cool toy, huh?

Let's get to it.

THE EXERCISE:

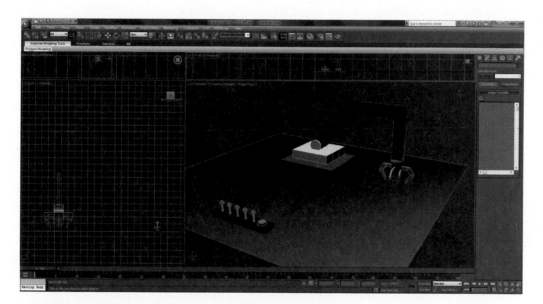

- Load the "crane-start.max" file from the Chapter 3 folder.

The first step is to link the parts of the crane together. Remember, the order is VERY important!

- Select all four Claw objects and link them to the Claw base. This "connects" the parts so that when the Claw base moves, so will the Claws. However, the Claws can move independently from the Claw base.

Let's finish up the linking of the crane, linking parts from the end of the crane, back towards the base.

- Select the Claw base and link it to Arm 3.

- Select Arm 3 and link it to Arm 2.

- Select Arm 2 and link it to Arm 1.

- Select Arm 1 and link it to the Turret.

- Select the Turret and link it to the Base. At this point, you should test to see if the linking worked properly. Select and rotate the Base on its Local Z Axis. Does the rest of the crane rotate with it? If so, you are ready for the next step.

- Select all the objects in the scene, and then [Alt]+right-click and choose "Freeze Rotation." This will, as described above in the Terms and Concepts, give us a zero point to set up rotational wiring to control the crane arm.

- Save your file now. Working with wiring can be a bit confusing at times. Save your work as you progress, too. Once a wired connection is made, and tested, save it.

Let's get the control pad working!

- Select "Control Stick 1," right-click and choose "Wire Parameters > Transform > Rotation > Keyframe XYZ > X Rotation." You should see a dotted line, like a rubber band that follows your cursor. Move your cursor over the "Turret" (tool tips should pop up to help you be sure you are wiring to the turret). Click on the "Turret" and choose "Transform > Rotation > Keyframe XYZ > Y Rotation."

The Parameter Wiring Dialog opens, and should look like the figure below.

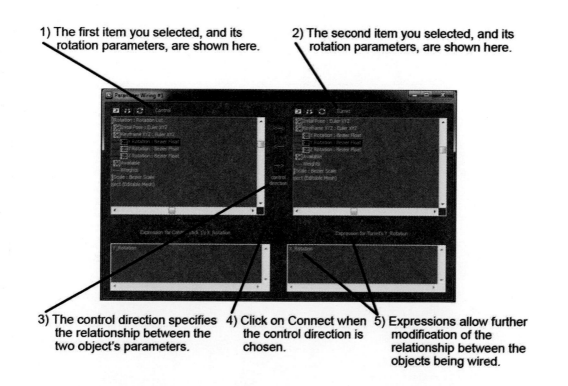

1) The first item you selected, and its rotation parameters, are shown here.

2) The second item you selected, and its rotation parameters, are shown here.

3) The control direction specifies the relationship between the two object's parameters.

4) Click on Connect when the control direction is chosen.

5) Expressions allow further modification of the relationship between the objects being wired.

NOTES

The Parameter Wiring Dialog is fairly straightforward. On the left is the first object we chose (Control Stick 1), and the parameter we chose to use (X Rotation). On the right is the second object we chose (Turret), and the parameter we chose to wire to (Y Rotation). In between the objects, are the "control direction" buttons. These buttons allows us to choose which object controls which.

- In this case, we will choose the right-pointing arrow, which will indicate the Control Stick 1 is controlling the Turret, as a one way connection.

- Once the control direction is specified, the "Connect" button becomes active. Click it to make the connection, but do not close the dialog box yet!

Since the Control Stick will only rotate about 90 degrees on its X axis before clipping the Control Base, we need to multiply the rotation of the Turret by 4 so that Control Stick 1 will be able to spin the Turret a full 360 degrees.

- In the "Expression for Turret's Y_Rotation" area, change the expression from "X_Rotation" to "(X_Rotation)*4" and click "Update."

NOTE: Be sure to turn on the Autokey button when you want to save animation. Also be sure to turn it off when you are done! MAX will not save any animation without the Autokey button on, and will animate any parameter changes when it is on!

You should now have a working control to rotate the Turret. The next steps are simply repeating the process for the other controls and crane parts.

- Select "Control Stick 2," right-click, choose "Wire Parameters > Transform > Rotation > Keyframe XYZ > X Rotation", then click on "Arm 1" and choose "Transform > Rotation > Keyframe XYZ > Y Rotation."

- When the Parameter Wiring window opens, select the arrow button that will make "Control Stick 2" control "Arm 1," and select "Connect." Test the behavior, and adjust the angle multiplier as before, if necessary. If you do add an expression after testing, be sure to click "Update."

- Test the wired parameter by rotating Control Stick 2 BEFORE closing the window.

- Select "Control Stick 3," right-click, choose "Wire Parameters > Transform > Rotation > Keyframe XYZ > X Rotation" then click on "Arm 2" and choose "Transform > Rotation > Keyframe XYZ > Z Rotation."

- When the Parameter Wiring window opens, select the arrow button that will make "Control Stick 3" control "Arm 2," and select "Connect." Test the behavior, and adjust the angle multiplier as before, if necessary. If you do add an expression after testing, be sure to click "Update."

- Test the wired parameter by rotating Control Stick 3 BEFORE closing the window.

NOTES

- Select "Control Stick 4" and right-click, choose "Wire Parameters > Transform > Rotation > Keyframe XYZ > X Rotation" then click on "Arm 3" and choose "Transform > Rotation > Keyframe XYZ > Z Rotation".

- When the Parameter Wiring window opens, select the arrow button that will make "Control Stick 4" control "Arm 3", and select "Connect". Test the behavior, and adjust the angle multiplier as before, if necessary. If you do add an expression after testing, be sure to click "Update".

- Test the wired parameter by rotating Control Stick 4 BEFORE closing the window.

- Select "Control Stick 5" and right-click, choose "Wire Parameters > Transform > Rotation > Keyframe XYZ > X Rotation then click on "Claw 1" and choose "Transform > Rotation > Keyframe XYZ > Z Rotation"

- When the Parameter Wiring window opens, select the arrow button that will make "Control Stick 5" control "Claw 1", and select "Connect". Test the behavior, and adjust the angle multiplier as before, if necessary. If you do add an expression after testing, be sure to click "Update".

- Test the wiring parameter, and DO NOT CLOSE THE WIRE PARAMETER DIALOG!

Notice that when you rotate "Control Stick 5" forward, the claw opens. It would make more sense for the claw to close when the control stick was pushed forward, so let's add a negative sign in front of the expression:

- Change the Expression for Claw 1's Z_Rotation to $-(Z\_Rotation)$.

- Test the wiring parameter, then close the Parameter Wiring window.

- Repeat the wiring process for "Control Stick 5" by wiring it to "Claw 2", "Claw 3", and "Claw 4".

- Test the wired parameter by rotating "Control Stick 5" and making sure all claws close BEFORE closing the window.

- Select "Control Knob" and right-click, choose "Wire Parameters > Transform > Rotation > Keyframe XYZ > Z Rotation" then click on "Claw Base" and choose "Transform > Rotation > Keyframe XYZ > Z Rotation".

- When the Parameter Wiring window opens, select the arrow button that will make "Control Knob" control "Claw Base", and select "Connect". Test the behavior, and adjust the angle multiplier as before, if necessary. If you do add an expression after testing, be sure to click "Update".

- Test the wiring parameter then close Parameter Wiring window. You may want to fix the rotation direction of the Claw Base: Do you remember how?

- Save your file.

NOTES

SUMMARY

Wire Parameters is a very powerful tool. It allows you to connect object parameters that simple linking cannot. Wiring is a very methodical process that connects parameters of one object to another. It can also be used to connect one object's parameters to MANY other objects' parameters.

It is always advisable to test a wired parameter before closing the Wire Parameter Dialog. The reason is that you may need to change the direction, amplification, or other expressions to get the motion you desire. It's easier to find the connections and edit them before you close the dialog.

REVIEW QUESTIONS

- After you "freeze rotations," can you still access the original rotational information?
- Why do we freeze rotations?
- How does Wire Parameters differ from the Select and Link tool?
- Why do we use the Local Coordinate System when wiring?
- What other expression commands and operators can we use in the Wire Parameter dialog?

BEYOND THE BASICS

- Re-wire the crane using only 2 control sticks. Remember, each rotational axis can be wired to different things.

- Apply a dull red material to the teapot in the crane exercise. Wire the twisting motion of one of the control stick to the material's specular level. You should be able to change the teapot from dull to shiny by twisting the stick. Can you think of other parameters you can wire to?

NOTES

CHAPTER FOUR

ANIMATING CAMERAS AND LIGHTS

PREVIEW

In this chapter, we will investigate the different uses of cameras in an animation. Cameras are the viewer's eyes, and you are free to guide them any way you want. The camera is used to tell the story.

Lights and their parameters are easy to animate, and there are many lighting features of MAX that can be very useful in our animations. Lights set the mood in our animations, and the placement and animation of them is as important as the motion you are animating.

TERMINOLOGY AND CONCEPTS

Cinematography: Usually defined as the art of composing and recording moving images with a camera. Think of the camera as a way of guiding the viewer through a scene. It is left up to you to tell the story you desire, by composing shots and taking your viewer through a story with the camera.

Rule of Thirds: A guideline for composing interesting and compelling images. The rule of thirds refers to placing objects of interest on lines which divide the scene into thirds in both vertically and horizontally.

Safe frames: Areas of the image, or scene, which are defined as safe for viewing on a television. Safe frames help avoid problems with objects near the borders of an image appearing in the rendered frame, but not displaying on a television.

Depth of Field (DOF): The distance between the closest and farthest objects in an image that are in focus. Depth of Field can also be thought of as focus effect which allows the main object of interest to remain in focus, while the foreground and background are blurry.

Multiplier (light parameter): The multiplier value of a light is the intensity of a light.

Sunlight system: A light system in MAX that uses geographically correct data and sun movement information to place a light in a scene. The time, date, and other parameters are animatable.

HANDS ON:
CINEMATOGRAPHY:

In the film industry, the cinematographer controls the look of the film as he sees it through the lens of a camera. Whether you are making a feature length film, short film, television commercial, taking still photos, or animating a bouncing ball for a lab grade in high school, you have to understand the basics of cinematography.

RULE OF THIRDS:

When I was young, long before digital cameras were even dreamed of, pictures were taken with cameras that exposed film to light. After a holiday, where the hundreds of camera flashes left my brothers and I blind for a month, we would get the pictures back from the developer to see if dad cut anyone's head off in the pictures. Although we were laughing at him, my father understood that the best pictures did not stick the subject in the center of the frame. What is the moral of this story? Listen to your . . . , I mean, frame your shots, do not just center them!

Framing your subjects in a visually interesting manner, whether in family photos or feature films, is very important. One rule to guide you in the right direction is the "Rule of Thirds." Look at the figure below.

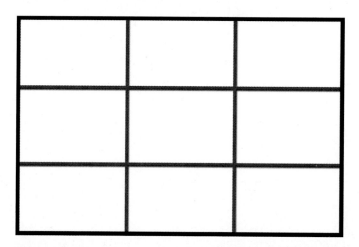

If you break up the image in the viewfinder, or in the MAX camera viewport, into thirds horizontally and vertically, you will have a clear picture of how to frame your shots. Let's look at a few examples.

NOTES

If you were going to take a picture of a beautiful sunset at a beach in Mexico, how would you frame it?

The main subject matter, or objects of interest, should be set on the lines. In this case, I would put the horizon line on the bottom third, and the trees on the left third. Okay, but what about using the Rule of Thirds with objects in motion? Open the "ROT-teapot.avi" file from the Chapter 4 folder on the CD-ROM.

If you were going to use a video camera to shoot a moving object, how would you frame the shot?

If the object was moving from left to right, such as the teapot in our example, you would frame the teapot in the left third (frames 10 and 25 in the figure below). You want to lead the action of the moving object. When the teapot returns, it moves from right to left, so you want to frame the teapot on the right third (frames 70 and 85 in the figure below.)

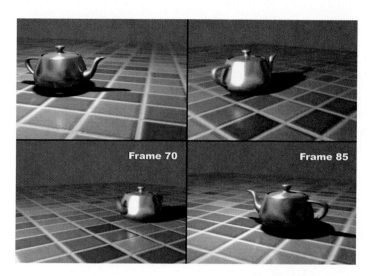

EXERCISE #1

- Open "dof-start.max" from the Chapter 4 folder on the CD-ROM. The scene is a very simple cityscape, with a red UFO animated to fly towards the camera. The camera's target is linked to the animated UFO.

We are going to experiment with a camera effect called Depth of Field (DOF). DOF describes how much of an image is in focus in relation to the main subject. Look at the image below, a rendering of the last frame of this exercise.

NOTES

The UFO and the buildings around it are in sharp focus. Those buildings in the background and foreground are out of focus. This DOF effect can be very useful in an animation or still rendering, to focus the viewer in on the main subject. It also adds a very artistic touch, similar to what people are used to seeing in film.

- Select "Camera01" and then right-click in the Camera01 viewport to activate it.

- Right-click on the Camera01 viewport label to open the "Viewport right-click Menu" and click on "Show Safe Frames."

You should see the Camera01 viewport change in aspect ratio, and have yellow, cyan and orange rectangles near the edges of the image. See the figure below.

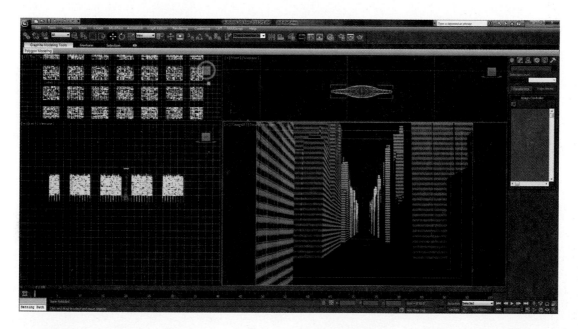

The yellow rectangle shows you the border of the image, as it will render with the current Render Dialog box settings of 640x480. The cyan rectangle is called the "action safe" border. The orange rectangle is called the "title safe" border.

The yellow border is useful when rendering to any format or medium. It shows you EXACTLY what will render with your current settings. The action safe area (cyan rectangle) helps you deal with overscan. Overscan is a built-in error correction which wastes pixels on a television display to ensure we see the screen completely filled from edge to edge. If anything you want the viewer to see is inside the action safe area, you are guaranteed that a viewer's television screen is displaying it. The orange rectangle is a guide to ensure titles are displayed nicely on the screen. Any text you are using as movie titles, information footers (like in a newscast), etc. should be kept within this area.

NOTES

- Move your cursor over the border between the viewports and the command panels, left-click and drag the panel to the left. This will give us more room to see the options in the command panels. See the figure below.

- At the bottom of the Parameters roll-out, you will see a section called "Multi-Pass Effect." Click to Enable these effects, make sure the Camera01 viewport is active, and press the "Preview" button.

You should see the viewport generate a preview of the DOF effect, with the current DOF Parameters.

With experience, you will be able to judge the quality of the DOF effect from the preview in the viewport. In our case, the effect is too strong. Let's look at how to improve it.

In the Depth of Field Parameters roll-out, you have two parameters which we will use to make the image better: Sample Radius and Dither Strength. The Sample Radius controls how much the scene gets shifted in the camera to generate the DOF effect. The Dither Strength controls how much grain is added to blend the passes.

- To improve the effect, set the Sample Radius to 0.25" and Dither Strength to 0.2". Click on the Preview button again, and compare this with the default settings. These new settings give less blur, and less grain.

- Move your Time Slider to frame 100, and click the Preview button again. Do you see the DOF change?

- Save your file.

Let's review what we did.

MAX cameras have the ability to generate both motion blur and DOF effects in their parameters in the modify panel. Both of these camera effects can be previewed in the viewport, saving a lot of rendering time.

These camera effects are generated "per-pass," or by rendering the file many times. By default, the Total Passes are set to 12. The more passes you designate, the better the quality of the effect. However, as with anything we do in 3D, higher quality means longer render times. As a test, go ahead and render a single frame of the animation from your saved file and watch what happens.

NOTES

Another aspect of the DOF effect was already set for you. The camera's target was linked to the animated UFO, and the default effect settings calculate DOF based upon the camera target location (under the "Depth of Field" Parameters, Focal Depth).

LIGHTING

Since this book is targeted towards animation, you should already be familiar with lights and lighting your scenes. However, some lighting features in MAX are geared towards animation. Two such features are the Sunlight and Daylight systems. Both Sunlight and Daylight systems work from a geographically correct location on earth, and calculate the position of the sun in the sky at any time, date, longitude and latitude. The Daylight System's lighting is based upon MAX's photometric lighting, and use of Light Tracer or Radiosity. To save render times for this exercise, we will study only the Sunlight System.

This exercise uses the Sunlight system to perform a useful task in the architectural design field: Lighting studies. For instance, if you have lot on which you plan to build your house, what would the best position to place your house to take advantage of light, solar heating, shadows, etc.?

- Open "sunlight-start.max" from the Chapter 4 folder on the CD-ROM. You will notice we have a simple house, garage, and a few trees.

- Go to the "Create > Systems" tab on the command panel. Chose "Sunlight" and go to the top viewport. Click in the center of the lot and drag outwards. Release the mouse to set the diameter of the Compass Rose. You are not done! Continue to create the system by dragging the mouse up and setting the position of the Sun01 light.

What we have just created is a compass which we can rotate to set the North direction. The Sun01 light is a direct light that acts like the sun in our sky. If you select the Sun01 light and go to the modify panel, you will see that it has Ray Traced Shadows enabled.

- With the Sun01 light still selected, go to the modify panel. This is where we will set the parameters of the sunlight system. See the figure below.

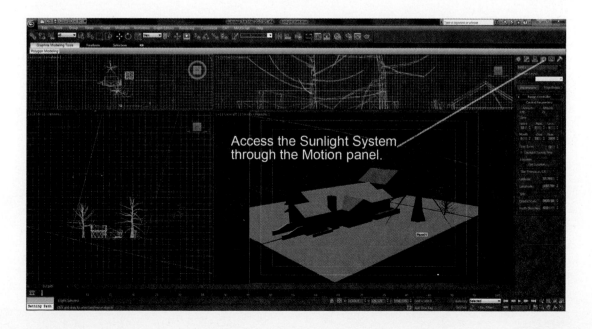

Access the Sunlight System through the Motion panel.

NOTES

- In the Control Parameters roll-out, go to the Orbital Scale spinner. Increase the value to around 3000 units. This will pull the light further away from the scene.

- Click the "Get Location . . . " button, and the Geographical Location dialog opens. See below.

- You can choose a location from the list on the left, or simply click on the map to choose the location you desire. Once you have chosen a location, click OK.

Notice that you could have also typed-in the latitude and longitude in the fields below the Get Location button.

- In the Time section of the Control Parameters, you can use the spinners or type in what time of day you would like to show. You can also set the date. Let's set the time to be 1:00 p.m., July 4, 2002. Notice that the time value is based upon a 24-hour clock, so 1:00 p.m. is 13 hours, 0 minutes, 0 seconds. Render a still frame, and see how the shadows fall almost straight down. Is that what you would expect?

- Select the Sun01 light again, and return to the motion panel. Set the time of day to 4:00 a.m., July 4, 2002. Your viewport should turn dark, as it is only 4 in the morning!

- Move your Time Slider to frame 100, and turn on the Autokey button. Set the time of day to be 10:00 p.m. (22 hours). Turn off the Autokey button, and drag the Time Slider to preview what you have created. To see this rendered from Boise, Idaho, open the file "sunlight-finished.avi" in the Chapter 4 folder on the CD-ROM.

- Save your file.

SUMMARY

Cameras animate like any other object in MAX. Cameras have some special animatable features, like DOF, to mimic photographic effects. Cameras in MAX have settings and parameters to match real-world cameras in most every way.

The Sunlight System is used for lighting studies, and lets you accurately place your scene in a geographically correct orientation with accurate sun placement.

NOTES

REVIEW QUESTIONS

- Can you animate the motion of a camera by using the camera viewport controls?
- What is DOF, and can the DOF parameters be animated?
- If I wanted to create a dimmer switch, I would use wire parameters to wire a switch's motion to what light parameter?
- How do you change the direction of North in a Sunlight System?
- What is "orbital scale" referring to in a Sunlight System?
- Why does a Sunlight System use a Direct light instead of a Spot light?

BEYOND THE BASICS

- Animate a dimmer switch using Wire Parameters.

- Create a clock. Using Wire Parameters, make the minute hand control the hour hand. Wire the clock to a Sunlight System. You should be able to rotate the minute hand of the clock to move the Sunlight.

- Animate a camera flying through a city. Use DOF to guide the viewer's focus to certain buildings as you fly by them.

NOTES

CHAPTER FIVE

ANIMATING ENVIRONMENTAL EFFECTS

PREVIEW

Effects are the sexy part of animation. Rather than rigging, wiring, modeling something with accuracy and detail, effects are "icing on the cake."

In this chapter, we will learn about making fire effects, volume lights, and motion blur. In a production environment, effects are one of the last things added to animation.

TERMINOLOGY AND CONCEPTS

Atmospheric Apparatus: A "bounding box" for environment effects like Fire and Volume Fog. There are three types of Atmospheric Apparatus: BoxGizmo, SphereGizmo, and CylGizmo.

Effects Panel: The panel in the Environment and Effects dialog where you set the parameters and options for effects like Fire, Volume Lights, and Volume Fog. The Environment and Effects dialog is accessed through the Rendering pull-down menu.

Phase: The Phase parameter controls the internal churning of the flames in the fire effect.

Drift: The parameter that controls the flame movement along the Z axis of the apparatus in a fire effect. High values give you a hotter-burning fire.

Volume Light: An environmental effect of a light that simulates the beam of light interacting with fog, smoke, or other atmospheric phenomena.

Motion Blur: A rendered MAX camera effect that simulates a real camera blurring the image of an object that moves while the shutter is open. Motion blur is a critical technique to add realism to your animations.

NOTES

HANDS ON:
EXERCISE #1

- Open "fire-start.max" from the Chapter 5 folder on the CD. We are going to create a campfire!

- In the Create Tab of the command panels, go to the Helpers button. We do not want a Standard helper, so pull down the list box and choose Atmospheric Apparatus. For a campfire, we will be using a "SphereGizmo."

- Click on the SphereGizmo button, and use the Top viewport to drag a SphereGizmo to the diameter of the fire ring (about 60 units).

- With the SphereGizmo still selected, go to the modify panel. We only need half of this sphere, so choose the "Hemisphere" option.

- Use the Select and Scale button on the main toolbar. Scale the gizmo vertically to about twice its current height. You should have a file similar to the figure below.

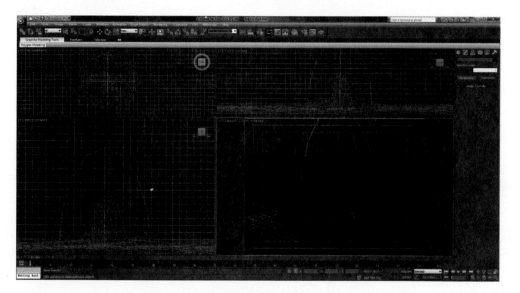

- With the SphereGizmo selected, go to the modify panel and the "Atmospheres & Effects" roll-out. Click the "Add" button. Choose "Fire Effect," and click "OK." You will see the Fire Effect added to the list of Atmospheres & Effects.

- Highlight the Fire Effect we just added, and then click "Set-up." The Environment and Effects dialog box will open up, and will look like the figure on the top of the next page.

- To see the Fire Effect Parameters, you will need to pan down in this dialog box. You can also close the roll-outs for Common Parameters and Exposure Control to help you see things better.

The first thing you will notice in the Fire Effect Parameters roll-out is the Gizmos section. Because we added the effect to the gizmo in the modify panel, the effect already knows which gizmo to apply the effect to.

NOTES

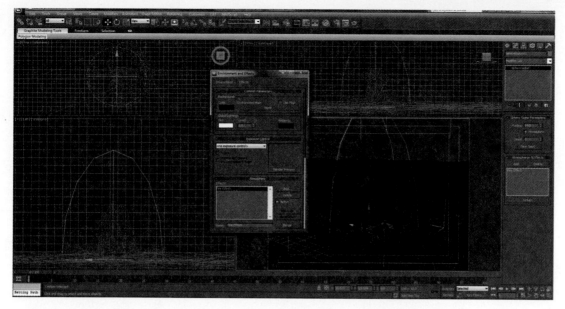

The next section is "Colors." We are trying to build a campfire, so the default colors will work just fine. If you were trying for a "Bunsen burner" type of flame from your high-school chemistry lab, you could change the colors to light and dark blue.

The Shape section is where we decide the general shape and direction of the flames we want.

- Choose a Tendril flame shape, and change the Stretch Value to 1.2 and the regularity to 0.3.

The Tendril type flame will make the tendrils orientate themselves to the local Z axis. In the case of a hemispherical gizmo, the local Z axis is upwards. The stretch value scales the tendrils of the flame along the local Z axis. Values greater than 1 stretch the flames, less than 1 squash the flames flat. Regularity is a measure of how much the flames fill the apparatus. Values approaching 1 will be "packed" into the apparatus, and the flames have little fading effect toward the edge of the apparatus.

The Characteristics section is where we set the flame size and appearance.

- Change the Flame Size to 20, and set the density to 25, Flame Detail to 10, and the Samples to 4.

The Flame Size is the size of the "internal flames" inside the apparatus. The Flame Detail controls the change from the inner to outer color we have set. The higher the value of detail, the sharper the edges and gradient between the colors become. Lower values add a soft look to the flames. The Density setting is for setting the opacity or "heat" of the flames. Lower values produce less opaque, low-temperature flames, while higher values become opaque and very "hot" looking.

NOTES

- Render the Camera01 viewport to see what we have set up. You should see a nice dense-looking flame around the logs. It should look like the image below.

If you were to render an AVI of the fire at this point, it would not move. To animate the fire effect, we need to animate settings in the Motion section of the Fire Effect Parameters.

- Move your Time Slider to frame 100, and turn on the Autokey button. Be sure you can still see the Motion section of the Fire Effect Parameters. At frame 100, change the value of the Phase to 200 and the Drift to 200. By default, MAX will fit a curve through these two keyframes. To make the fire burn uniformly, go to the curve editor and change the Phase and Drift keyframes to Linear tangency. Take note of where the Fire Effect is located in the Curve Editor! See the figure below.

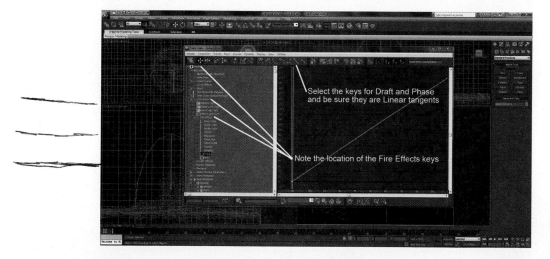

Sometimes MAX does not display the environmental effects by default. To enable their display, you will want to do the following:

- Open the curve editor, and click on the Filters icon (see the figure on the next page)

- Click the radio box on the left (as shown) to enable the display of "Global Tracks"

- Click "OK"

NOTES

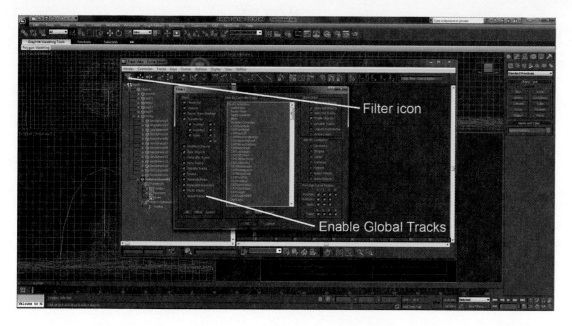

You should now have the expanded Curve Editor display showing the Environment section. Expand it to show the Fire Effect, as shown.

- Save your file.

- Render the time segment to an AVI file, or look at the finished render, "fire-finished.avi" in the Chapter 5 folder on the CD.

The fire effect in MAX is only an effect. It does not light your scene, or cast shadows. Lights would need to be added to the scene, and then their color changed and multipliers animated to obtain a more lifelike scene.

In addition, you need to be aware that fire and other effects need to be rendered from a perspective viewport, or camera viewport. Top, left, and other orthogonal or orthographic viewports will not render the effect.

EXERCISE #2

In this exercise, we will create a spooky night scene using a volume light.

- Open the "volumelight-start.max" file from the Chapter 5 folder on the CD-ROM.

In the scene, there is a banyan tree in a valley, with a bright moon in the sky. We will add the filtered light rays that the moon would create if it were a foggy night.

- Select "spot-moonlight" and go to the modify panel. Near the bottom of the modify panel, you will find the "Atmospheres & Effects" roll-out. Click on the "Add" button, and choose Volume Light. Click "OK."

- In the Atmospheres & Effects list, click on the Volume Light, and click the "Set-up" button.

NOTES

Just as with the Fire Effect, the Environment and Effects dialog box opens. Close some of the roll-outs, or pan down to see the Volume Light Parameters roll-out.

- Without changing any of the parameters, render the scene. You should see something like the image below.

As with the fire effect, volume lights only render in a perspective or camera viewport. As you can see, we are getting the foggy look from our spotlight, but it is too "dense." Good thing there's a Density setting . . .

- Change the Density to 1, and re-render the scene. The render should look like the image below.

NOTES

- To add some depth to the fog in the volume light, we can use the Noise section. Turn on "Noise" with the checkbox, change the amount to 0.6, the Type of noise to Fractal and the size to 40. This will break up the uniform fog, and should look like the image below.

Add some interest to the image by making the fog of the volume light move a little.

- Turn on the autokey button, and move the time slider to frame 100. Set the Phase value to 5.

- Open the Curve Editor and change the Phase curve tangents to linear, as shown below.

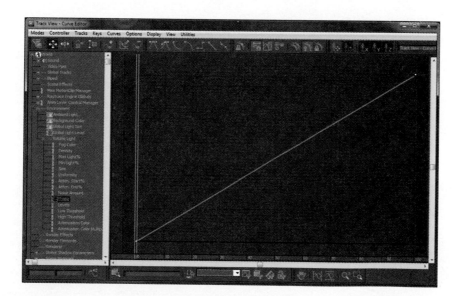

- Save your file.

- Render the animation, or view the finished render "volumelight-finished.avi" in the Chapter 5 folder on the CD-ROM.

NOTES

EXERCISE #3

Motion Blur is one of those effects that is easily overlooked by the novice animator. Motion Blur does not look very appealing when you look at a still frame, but when you render an animation, it is vital to the realism of the scene.

There are many ways to accomplish motion blur: image motion blur, object motion blur, multi-pass camera effect motion blur, motion blur effect, and scene motion blur in video post.

No matter how you do it, just use it.

The first motion blur we are going to try is Image Motion Blur.

- Open "cameralogo-start.max" from the Chapter 5 folder on the CD-ROM. The file has a logo with an animated camera.

- Select "Plane01," "Text01," and "Text02," and right-click to open the Quad Menu. Choose Properties, and you should see the dialog box below.

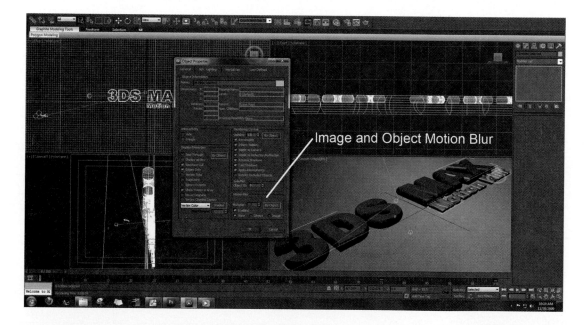

Image and Object Motion Blur

- This is where you enable Image or Object Motion Blur. Note that although the blur is "enabled" by default, no blur is applied due to the None checkbox being checked.

- Click to enable Image Motion Blur.

NOTES

- Open the Render Dialog box from the Rendering pull-down menu, main toolbar, or simply hit [F10]. In the render dialog box, click on the "Renderer" tab. Pan down to the bottom of the dialog box, and you should see what is shown below.

- Since we have enabled Image Motion Blur, only the image Motion Blur setting will apply. Set the Duration (frames) to 1.

For all types of Motion Blur, there will be a duration setting. With a duration setting of 1, the image will be blurred over the distance that the object moves in a single frame.

- Render the animation, or view the file "motionblur-IMG.avi" from the Chapter 5 folder on the CD.

Image Motion Blur is the fastest blur to render. This is due to the fact that the blur is added after the image is rendered. Image Motion Blur takes camera movement into account. Image Motion Blur can cause problems with particles and with objects interacting with transparent or refractive materials.

- Re-select "Plane01," "Text01," and "Text02," and right-click to open the Quad Menu. Choose Properties, and change Object motion blur to None.

This will disable any other motion blur effects to isolate the Camera Multi-Pass blur.

- Select Camera01, and go to the modify panel. Enable the Multi-Pass Effect.

- Change the Bias to 0.6, and set the Dither Strength to 0.17.

The Bias setting of greater than 0.5 (default) moves the blur behind the object a bit. The Dither Strength setting was dropped from the default of 0.4 to make the effect less grainy.

- Render the animation, or view the file "motionblur-MPC.avi" from the Chapter 5 folder on the CD-ROM.

NOTES

SUMMARY

Motion blur recreates the effect we see in photos and video where fast-moving objects blur the film while the shutter is open. There are many ways to generate motion blur in MAX, including Object, Image, and Camera Multi-Pass motion blur.

The Fire Effect in MAX can create fairly convincing flames. By using the effect settings, you can create everything from small campfires to a large fireball explosion. Phase and Drift parameters are used to animate the fire effects.

Volume Lights create the effect of a light beam interacting with atmospheric phenomena. You have seen this effect used in film with flashlight beams, car headlights, and moonlight effects.

REVIEW QUESTIONS

- What is used to define the volume of a Fire Effect?
- In a Tendril flame, which axis will the tendrils have when using a BoxGizmo? CylGizmo? SphereGizmo?
- What effect will the "Samples" have on a tendril flame?
- What Fire parameters should be used to animate flames?
- Why do you need Linear tangents on the Phase and Drift keyframes?
- What types of lights can we use Volume Light effects with?
- How are Object and Image motion blur activated for objects?
- What does the "duration" setting mean when using motion blur?

BEYOND THE BASICS

- Add a few trees and a picnic table to the campfire scene. Animate a light to simulate the flickering light of the fire.

- Create a large building. Animate a fire consuming the building. What settings were different for this fire when compared to the campfire?

- Animate a car traveling down a road at a high rate of speed. Use volume lights for the headlights, and motion blur to the scene. What light parameters will limit the distance of the headlights, so they do not shine too far down the road?

NOTES

CHAPTER SIX

PUTTING IT ALL TOGETHER

PREVIEW

You should now feel comfortable with animating in MAX, and undoubtedly have many ideas bouncing around in your head. Hopefully, one or more of the exercises in this book have inspired an idea for a larger project. So how do we get there?

This chapter guides you through the entire process, from developing the idea through sketches, storyboards, and all the way to the final render. We will not be making *The Incredibles* here, but rather more of a short animation showing your skills: A demo reel piece of 15 seconds to 1 minute long.

TERMINOLOGY AND CONCEPTS

Brainstorming: Generating ideas. Brainstorming is the first step in starting your project.

Story Development: What is going to happen in your animation? What are you trying to show? How are you going to convey the ideas, or demonstrate the process? This is where you have to hold the interest of the viewers and make them want to watch.

Art Design: Art design consists of sketches of the objects and locations in your animation. For inspiration, take a look at books such as *The Art of Star Wars, Episode II—Attack of the Clones* by Mark Cotta Vaz (Compiler). The sketches and paintings you will see will give you an idea of how much work goes into the design before the mouse hits the pad. The drawings of the landscapes, buildings and ships in the movie are wonderful examples of designing everything in a scene to look as if it belongs to the same world. Do the objects in your scene look like they belong together?

Storyboards: Storyboards are the plan for the animation. It may help to think of a comic book or comic strip in the Sunday newspaper. Storyboards are a shot-by-shot sketch of all the action and movement in a scene. It should contain well-balanced and composed shots, action lines, sounds, camera motions, atmosphere, etc.—anything that explains what is happening. Storyboards should contain enough information for anyone to understand what to animate and how to create your vision.

Production: This is the phase that so many beginners rush into. This phase involves modeling your objects, adding materials, lights and cameras, and animating the scenes. The production phase should always be based upon the ideas, art design, story development, and storyboards.

Editing and Post Production: In the post production and editing phases, problems are fixed, sounds are added, music is scored, effects are rendered. Editing involves taking all the shots, and the storyboards, and making the story flow. Transitions are added, timing worked out, and sometimes scenes are deleted. Some basic editing functions can actually be done in MAX's Video Post, but most of the time editing software such as Premiere and Final Cut are better suited to the task.

NOTES

HANDS ON:
BRAINSTORMING:

For some people, brilliant ideas for an animation are always available. For the rest of us, they can take some time to develop. Inspiration can come from anywhere, and we have to recognize when the ideas come, and write them down.

Brainstorming is a very valuable step in developing an idea for an animation. You may find it very helpful to have a group of people assist in this process. Brainstorming is the process of generating ideas. Anything goes in this phase, and no limitations should be imposed. Write down any ideas people may have, because you never know what ideas may inspire new ones. Keep generating these ideas until they are all exhausted. If you do not have a group to work with, this phase should take place over a period of time. This will allow you to write down inspired ideas as they come to you, wherever and whenever they occur.

Once you have the raw ideas down on paper, it is time to sort them. Ideas should be combined, evaluated, and sorted into lists to try and hone in on one coherent story. Be careful to consider the limits of modeling and animation time, as well as render time. Be sure to also consider the depth of your knowledge and skills. Some people (myself included) find that their best work happens when they are pulled out of their comfort zone. However, being in way over your head isn't a pleasant feeling! You have to find balance and gauge whether you have the time to learn what you do not feel comfortable with.

STORY:

In any project, whether a short film or television commercial, the story is what makes the project successful. If you are generating ideas on your own, or in a group as discussed above, then you should have some ideas that can be used to develop a story. Keep your story simple, and based upon something that most people can identify with.

The first step in story development will be to identify your intended audience. Your brainstorming sessions should suggest an intended audience, along with the subject matter chosen. For example, if you are animating a car engine for a commercial about motor oil, your audience is mostly adult males.

When your audience is defined, you need to develop story ideas focusing on grabbing the audience and keeping their attention. How do you make the audience remember your product? You need additional images, sounds, and narration that support the main idea and fill out the story.

Keeping with the motor oil idea, you may want to use images of fast cars, big trucks, revving engine sounds, and a well-designed oil label. The story will center on the durability and protective aspects of the oil, and try to make the viewer think your oil is best.

Story is still important with a short 15-second long demo reel. The story in this case can be as simple as a gag or joke. Use a subject matter that is interesting and can easily identified with by your audience.

ART DESIGN:

Now that you know what elements you need to use, it's time to find a quiet place and break out the sketchbook and pencils. Yes, that's right—PENCILS! Those of you who say you cannot draw just have not drawn enough to get better at it. You should be practicing any chance you can. The process of sketching out ideas is a highly creative one, which is valuable beyond the actual artwork you are creating. While you are sketching, your mind will begin to get very creative, and will start generating new ideas as you progress.

NOTES

Using the story and message you need to deliver, sketch some ideas for the objects in your scene. Try to develop a unique and interesting style that supports the ideas of the story. Experiment with many ideas and designs. You should be very open-minded here as well, just free sketching ideas.

Do not overlook the camera angles and surrounding environments in your scenes. Try developing the lighting and camera information while you are sketching. These will be very valuable later.

Once these ideas are on paper, sort through them in a similar manner as when you were brainstorming ideas. Find the sketches that are complementary to all that we have developed already with the story and audience.

STORYBOARDING:

Once your story ideas are set, it's time to pick up the pencils again. That's right, pencils! Sketching skills cannot be over emphasized here: Practice, practice, practice! Being able to draw can be critical to the success of your project in many ways.

Storyboarding is best described as creating a comic book of every aspect of your story. Storyboards are where the story becomes pictures: Camera angles should be defined, objects needed in the scene are sketched, background information drawn, and descriptions of lighting, motion, noises, music, and dialog provided. The storyboards should contain enough frames to accurately describe the actions and story so that any animator would know what he needed to do to complete the project. A storyboard layout I use is shown below. It is also on the CD-ROM, in the Chapter 6 folder.

Project: _____ Date:_____

Client: _____ Job#: _____

Shot # _____

Description:
_____
_____
_____

Shot # _____

Description:
_____
_____
_____

NOTES

Finally, storyboards are important for another reason: Progress payments! On almost every project I have worked on, the client required storyboards as an approval of the project. This approval almost always marked a progress milestone on the schedule and a paycheck.

PRODUCTION:

The production phase is where MAX is used! Modeling the objects and scenes according to the story and art design is the first step. Modeling needs to be done with a keen eye on how objects will be animated and interact with each other.

Once the models are built, you can move on to the material and lighting of the objects in the scenes. Keep the storyboards and artworks close at hand! These are your guides to the look and feel of the production.

The rigging of the objects should be the next phase. Assemble the scenes and get the objects ready to be animated. The main focus should be on how to make the animator's job easier. This is where the link constraints, path constraints, and wiring parameters are used. Again, focus on ease of use, and allowing the animator freedom to create the motion!

Animation is the final production phase of the project. Using the storyboards as a guide, the animator creates the story using the rigs and controls. The lighting and materials are finalized, and the scenes are rendered.

POST PRODUCTION AND EDITING:

Post Production and Editing is the final step in the process. All of the rendered scenes are assembled, along with sound effects, narration, music, and titles. Storyboards again are used as the guide.

Editing involves assembling the pieces into the whole story, and is a very creative and important phase of the project. The editor has to be able to understand timing of sequences to squeeze the right emotion from each scene. He also must be able to use transitions to make the user understand the passage of time, or change of scene.

REVIEW QUESTIONS

- Why should you sketch your ideas out on paper before modeling?
- What are the benefits of creating detailed storyboards?
- What phases of a project can benefit from thorough storyboards?
- Which part of the production process are you best suited for?

NOTES

BEYOND THE BASICS

Search for jobs in the animation industry using sites such as:

- www.cgsociety.org - sign up for a free account, participate in the forums and contests, and keep an eye on the jobs.
- www.monster.com
- www.awn.com

- What specific jobs are available in each production phase in this chapter?

- What are the job requirements? Software used?

- How many jobs require basic art skills and traditional art?

- Visit 3D art and animation sites such as:

  - www.3dtotal.com
  - www.cgsociety.org
  - www.cgchannel.com

  How does your work compare to the images in the galleries on these sites?

- Some of the links from lichiman.aniguild.com take you to personal websites of animators like Carlos Baena. Carlos works at Pixar, and is mentioned by name many times in the commentary by Brad Bird on *The Incredibles* DVD. What makes Carlos' work good enough to be hired by Pixar?

NOTES

INDEX